Mi
BAJA
No Hurry No Worry

Bernie Swaim

Caballero Publishing
Santee, California

Cover Design and Illustrations by Jerry Meloche
Meloche Enterprises.com

ISBN 0-9721863-0-1

Library of Congress Catalog
Card Number 2002092346

Caballero Publishing
PO Box 710411
Santee, California 92072-0411
http://www.caballeropublishing.com

DEDICATION

This book is dedicated to the memory of Art McLaren, the macho guy who introduced me to this wonderful land and its welcoming people.

He was at once my boss, mentor, and friend. He taught me to live with one foot in Baja and the other in San Diego.

SALUD!

Acknowledgements

To Lu Ann

My Little Lady who very early on
understood just what Baja really
meant to me.
She always recognized when my stress
level had built to a point
that a Baja trip
became a very necessary event.

A very large thanks to Jerry Meloche whose artwork and talents resulted in the cover and all of the illustrations throughout this book.

To "JC" Jim Callahan, whose technical assistance allowed this book to be born in print.

San Diego City Jail

I was first introduced to the Land of *Mañana* (dictionary says tomorrow—but it really just means NOT TODAY) early in April of 1964. I was a young hard charging rookie cop and Captain Art McLaren was a middle aged, hardnosed, boss from the old school. We all thought he was hard as nails and in routine conversation he conveyed that impression with his deep, almost a whisper, gravelly voice. But!—When he began talking about Baja California his voice mellowed out and his shoulders relaxed a bit. He was a large heavy boned Scotsman who delighted in becoming involved in new and different experiences. When he got caught up in his Love Affair with Baja he didn't just wade in—he jumped into the culture and became very concerned with its people.

Over coffee one morning he told us about his efforts to secure corrective surgery for a young man from La Mision. Pepe was about fourteen years old and was a fairly handsome young guy except he had a cleft palate that detracted from his looks and caused the other kids to tease him. Art told us that he had arranged for a team of doctors to donate their skills for *nada* (nothing) and Scripps Hospital was willing to provide care for Pepe. The largest problem was getting his parents to agree to let their son go 'north'. Next was getting through all of the paperwork that both governments required. Art laughed and said, "I'm used to getting past bureaucrats. That's what I do for a living."

A few days later Mac asked me if I would like to wander down to La Salina with him. I jumped at the chance and as a result my life was changed forever. I fell in love with Baja <u>and</u> its people. I learned to live with one foot in the United States and the other in Mexico. Years later I developed a very strong desire to capture the magic, humor, the fun, and yes, the sadness too, of this small campo nestled on the shores of the Pacific Ocean just a few miles south of the San Diego.

Over the years I have read many books about Baja, but with the exception of "God and Mr. Gomez" by Jack Smith, most of them only addressed HUNTING, FISHING, and looking for new forms of cactus. No one had written about the Baja that a whole bunch of us crazy gringo's had discovered. We had come to Baja just looking for a place to get away from the 'rat race.' A place to just kick back and enjoy life! We soon found that it was a much more pleasant experience when we interacted with the happy, smiling, people who lived in our part of Baja—I know it is really not ours—but our new friends made us welcome. They taught us how to put together a *fiesta*, to eat, drink, dance, and enjoy each other's company. They taught us to slow down, to watch the sunrise and then to watch for the *green flash* as the sun slid into the Pacific.

Without saying it they showed us how to breathe to the rhythm of the crashing waves. To know that watches were really of no practical use in this *little bit of paradise.* That time was only your friend if you realized that its passage only added to your enjoyment of life. Getting older doesn't matter, it only matters that you live your life with your family and friends and that you extend your hand in friendship to all of the wonderful people around you.

These not so simple people taught us how to enjoy life! They nudged us into a better and more honest understanding of ourselves. They helped us to build our homes. They taught us to see much more than we previously could or would, to see and understand things that proved to be so much more meaningful and added so much to our lives.

Hopefully, in reading this book you will find that in a round about way it is a "How to Book on Living in Baja." You will learn how to build a house and to appreciate that it is a living thing. You will understand how to become a 'legal' alien in Mexico. How to acquire land. Notice that I did not say how to 'own' land. How to understand, work with, and enjoy the people that make this place what it is!

With the proper attitude, learning a different and more relaxing way of life will be so much fun. You will learn how to party at the drop of a hat. *AND* you will learn what is truly important in this life!

You will learn—THAT ONCE THE DUST OF BAJA SETTLES ON YOUR SHOULDERS YOU MAY NEVER SHAKE IT OFF.

A Whole New World

My first trip to La Salina Del Mar was with Art in his old beat up 1951 Ford pickup. It was a dull red in color; the right headlight was broken, and it had been driven quite aggressively. It carried battle scars from front to rear. It was one of those vehicles that always, without question, was given the right of way. Trash that covered the passenger's side of the truck had to be removed before I could get in. This revealed a large spring sticking out of the seat on the passenger's side. Art laughed and made a crude remark as I gingerly seated myself around the spring. We were off on my first adventure into Baja. I had been to Tijuana a few times but this was to be a trip to the 'interior' of Baja.

Our first stop was at a local market, in San Diego, where Art picked up a case of frozen chickens. The guy in the store knew Art and what he was going to do with the chickens so he gave him a 30% discount. We also bought a few green onions and some chicken livers, these and some

Mexican rolls proved to be our entire stock of food for our two-day trip.

In 1964 the first thing you saw after crossing the border was a squatter's camp that was home to hundreds of people. It stretched from the border gate, west along the border road, to about where the 'PRI' offices are now. A depressing sight! It consisted of shacks built of cardboard, old tires, and anything else that would help keep the weather out. The entire camp existed in a sea of mud and stagnate water. You rapidly realized that you were in a very different world. Kids were playing soccer with the ball sliding off into the mud. The camp had evolved as wave after wave of people from the interior trekked to Tijuana looking for a better life! The sheer number of squatters absolutely overwhelmed the town's ability to deal with the squalor. Finally, with the help of the Federal Government, the squatters were forcibly removed to a more sanitary and healthy location.

Down the road a bit we stopped at a liquor store that was just across from the old City Cemetery. Art went in and asked the owner for ten (10) cases of Corona beer. Corona at that time only cost a dime a bottle. Art shuffled through his wallet and handed the guy a <u>discount card</u> that entitled him to 10% off—so  we got 11 cases for the price of 10. I loaded the beer in, on, and around the already overloaded pickup while Art chatted with the owner.

As we dropped out of the hills, just north of Rosarito, Art pulled over next to a very old Indian man. He wore old threadbare pants with an old dirty blanket thrown over his slight shoulders; he wore old tire tread *zapatas* (sandals). He was carving a chunk of wood into what was beginning to look like an eagle. Art introduced me to the old guy. Then he and the Indian talked for a while. You should understand that he didn't speak much Spanish and the old guy didn't speak any English—and very little Spanish. A lot of the Indians could barely understand the official Mexican language. In spite of this both men seemed to really enjoy each other's company.

Eventually, Art picked up a small wooden whale and tossed it in his the truck. In payment he presented a pound box of lard to the old guy for the carving. They gave each other an *'Abrazo'* (hug) and we were off. Art noticed my confusion and explained that lard was a basic part of the Mexican diet and that it was very expensive and hard to find in Baja.

As we neared to Rosarito Beach Mac started sounding like a guy from the 'local chamber of commerce'. He began to extol the virtues of this dusty little town. The entire city was west of the current toll road and counted a mere 10,000 to 15,000 people of whom almost half were retired Americans. If you needed gas or booze this was your last chance until you hit Ensenada. Avenida Juarez *was* the only road south.

Driving down the old coast road in that old beat up truck with McLaren was a fascinating learning experience. It was just like being in school and getting a crash course on the history and people of this part of the world. It seemed as though he knew everyone we passed and they obviously knew that old red truck and its laughing driver.

Art never drove more than 45 miles an hour and most of the time we were only going about 20. We were always in third gear with the motor lugging down so badly that it seemed to be on the verge of stalling. When I asked him why he drove so slowly he just laughed and said, "That way you can see what's happening! That's the way the old truck likes to be driven—just slow and easy."

As we approached K-58 (all distances in Mexico are in kilometers) he pulled the truck off the highway and we bounced down onto an old, dusty rutted, dirt road. He announced that this road led into Campo Lopez where we would find two restaurants that served lobster tacos. He claimed that they were the best tacos in the whole world. Placing the truck in low gear we slowly made our way down to the first restaurant, which proved to be closed. A young man came by and told us that the place down on the point was open. We thanked him, backed up, and proceeded very slowly down the hill. It was here that I learned why Art always drove so slowly. His brakes were so worn that they were unable to even slow his truck!

Campo Lopez was, and still is, one of the most beautiful spots along the entire coast. It falls down and away from the highway and ends at a point where the Pacific Ocean crashes with white foam over the rock-strewn beach. The restaurant (no name) sits on a small bluff with a 180-degree view of the pounding surf. A large and lonely old palm tree reached for the sky right next to

15

the, small unpainted, building. We were pleased to find that it was open and 'Paco' said he would be happy to fix us some *langosta* burritos. He popped the lids on a couple of *Coronas* and told us that he would be back in *uno momento*. He was wearing the typical Mexican beach attire, a pair of cutoff Levi's, a straw hat, long, shiny black hair sticking out, and a broad white smile.

Enjoying my beer, I looked around and found the place to be quite clean in spite of the dirt floor. There were windows on all four walls that afforded us an exceptional view of the ocean on three sides; the fourth opened onto a hillside where numerous goats were eating everything in sight. Somehow it didn't surprise me that the windows contained no glass. An old wood burning stove dominated the room and the tables, two, were accompanied by benches that consisted of upturned coke cases with wooden boards for seats.

When we asked Paco for some burritos we received the sign, most people who have spent any time kicking around Baja have seen it, the hand in front of the speakers face with the thumb and index finger lightly touching. It is usually given with a verbal *uno momento* (in a minute). A couple of beers later we wandered down to the beach and found a young boy hauling a small, green and almost white boat up onto the rocks.

Laughing, he told us that Paco had just returned from his lobster traps with lobster for our *comida* (lunch).

No way can you get lobster fresher than that!

Returning to the restaurant we found Paco rolling great chunks of white lobster meat in huge flour tortillas. He placed them, four at a time, into a large black cast iron skillet. They were covered in bubbling butter. When they turned a golden brown he served each of us two burritos. *Estupendo!* (Wonderful!) We each had six burritos and a couple more beers. Amazingly, the total tab for a dozen lobster burritos and eight beers came to $5.00 US. One dollar for the food and four dollars for the beer. I have never had such a great meal. I think of it still!

Rolling on down the highway we passed "La Fonda's" and turned inland to La Mision. To get to La Salina you had to go into La Mision, turn right, cross over a small stream, and then climb up a bumpy dirt road that just hung on the side of the cliff. At the top you turned south and traveled about 1½ miles to the lagoon. Here you turned right and the next thing you saw was 'Rancho Benson's Bar' overlooking a beautiful, wide, white beach and the blue-blue Pacific Ocean. That was all there was to La Salina del Mar the first time I visited it.

Backing up for a minute before we crossed that stream we stopped off at the orphanage, which consisted of two old white washed adobe houses. Most of the windows were cracked or broken and one of the doors sagged on its hinges. The houses served as both a home and as classrooms during poor weather. Most of the instruction was conducted in the shade of a huge old tree.

When the kids heard Art's truck they came from everywhere, running, stumbling, and running some more to meet that beat up old red pickup and the guy who drove it. They knew Art always had chickens aboard and he usually had several bags of good used clothes, which he had collected from friends. The way they acted you would have thought that McLaren was Santa Claus.

When we entered the bar, Señor Benson and his son greeted Art with great affection. They nodded politely at me and then ignored me. Art ordered vodka rocks and I asked for a cold beer. We got vodka no ice and a warm Corona. Art visited with them for a while and then we headed for his lot. At that time there were NO houses or trailers in camp. The main road was just a dusty track through a field of those tall weeds with the pretty yellow flowers. I don't know their name but the goats won't even eat them. We only had about 200 yards to go to get to his lot. It took us over an hour to travel that short distance. He would drive 20 feet and the truck would become stuck in the soft sand. Art would take a pull on his beer, laugh, and direct me to, "Dig her out, boy."

This happened so many times that when we got to his place it was all I could do to pop a beer, lean against the fender, and rest. Later on we started using short lengths of rubber conveyer belts to keep from getting stuck! We brought down four 30-foot lengths of belt that we laid out, butted end to end along the road. Once the rear wheels of the truck had crossed onto the second set of belts we would drag the first set of the belts to the front of the truck. This process was continued until we got to Arts lot. This tedious process was always necessary because he always had his truck seriously overloaded! No! Letting air out of the tires never helped.

I rested through a couple of beers while listening to Art carry on about what a beautiful lot he had picked. He bought the first lot and built the first house in La Salina del Mar. It's the two story 'A' Frame that sits on the largest lot in camp.

We unloaded all of the building materials, tools, and beer before we started to settle down. It was getting close to dark so we lit a Coleman lantern and had another beer as we watched the sun slip into the Pacific. I've been watching that sun slide into the ocean for over 30 years and I have never gotten over how beautiful and final it is when it sinks.

Climbing into our sleeping bags we were soon settled in for the night. I lay there for while listening to the silence broken only by the waves crashing upon the beach. It seemed like only a few minutes passed before I awoke with the sun in my face and Art snoring in my ear. He drowned out the sound of the surf.

We had breakfast, green onions; cold fried chicken livers, *boleos*, and a beer. Don't get the wrong idea; McLaren never carried water to Baja until after the house was built. What a way to start the day, just sitting in the sun and listening to the surf.

I worked clearing the lot, while Art told stories of Baja. He didn't really work very hard but his stories were first class. He told me how he had met Jack Speer while he was working in downtown San Diego as a Police Sergeant. As the story goes they met while Jack was wandering around the city apparently lost and somewhat under the influence of demon rum. Instead of taking him to jail Art took him back to his motel. A friendship formed which was to last far beyond Jack's founding of the Campo at La Salina. He brought Art to La Salina, before the subdivision was even started. It still has not been completed over 30 years later. When Art picked the location for his lot he and Jack threw stones to the four corners of the lot to determine its limits. That's why McLaren's lot is so much larger that the standard lot in camp. Jack started selling (leasing) lots for $200.00 down and $25.00 per month for 30 years. That was the going price for a front, ocean view, lot from 1964 until about 1970.

We worked, wandered on the beach, drank, and dreamed until it was suddenly time to return to the real world. Before we left I stacked the beer, building materials, and tools. We covered them with a tarp. You might return in a week or a month but you never had to worry. They would still be there when you returned.

On our way back we stopped in Rosarito Beach where Art bought five gallons of *Oso Negro* (black bear) Vodka. I told him that I thought we could only take a quart apiece across the border, he just laughed, that funny laugh of his and said, "Just watch." He proceeded to pour all of the vodka into an empty five-gallon water bottle. Placing

20

the bottle in the corner of the bed he threw dirty clothes over it. When we got to the border the Customs guy asked him if he had anything to declare he just smirked and replied, "Just some dirty clothes." He did that for many years before he got caught and had to pay a very hefty fine.

Back to Baja

My second trip to La Salina started in much the same fashion as the first. I climbed into that beat up old truck, settled myself around that broken spring, and made myself comfortable. Art said that this trip would be a little different; we would be wandering around downtown Tijuana to buy a few things for the orphanage. I was not terrible excited about the idea of driving around "TJ" but I should not have worried. I found that not even Tijuana taxi drivers would mess with that old truck and its laughing driver. I just settled in and felt very safe.

Our first stop was at the produce market where Art bought a hundred pounds of beans and rice. I tossed them in the back of the truck; which was parked squarely in the middle of the street. Several people were yelling at Art to move his wreck. He just laughed and went about buying several kinds of vegetables; a few of which I had never seen. The colors, sounds, and smells of the market were *mucho* different and much more alive than those in the States. People would argue and scream and then they would laugh and slap each other on the back. Seeing this scene for the first time made me think that they were going to kill each other. In reality all they were doing was haggling over price.

Our purchases completed we wandered down some dirty back roads until we came to an old, falling down, ramshackle building. Art stopped, again, in the middle of the road. I followed him in and was surprised to find schoolbooks, pencils, and paper; dumped in bins all around the inside of the building. The books were all in Spanish but Art seemed to know exactly what he wanted. I thought he could read the titles. I found out later that the teachers at the orphanage had given him a 'wish' list.

Returning to the *Libre* (free road) we headed south over the mountain to Rosarito. Soon Art pulled into the La Gloria's Hotel and Bar. He explained that he felt that it was his duty to teach me something new about Baja every time he had a chance. We went in and he introduced me to a very proud Mexican man named Paulo. He was dressed in a shiny, threadbare, black suit. He had been a bartender at La Gloria's since its heydays when all of the Hollywood Stars stopped here while on their way further south to explore Baja (and to buy booze during prohibition). Pictures of Stars were all over the walls, Rita Hayworth, John Wayne, John Huston, etc, etc.

We had a drink, talked for a while, and then we were away.

The road down the mountain to Rosarito Beach was only one lane in each direction and it was full of curves. Trucks of all kinds were slowly ascending and descending at a snail's pace. This caused a whole lot of suicidal type behavior by drivers who would not be slowed by the trucks. This was my first exposure to the little white crosses with flowers at their bases; these crosses dotted the roadside all the way to Ensenada.

We waved at the old wood carver but we didn't stop! A short time later we pulled in at the Half-Way House and Art introduced me to a short, sloppy, fat, old man who had run the bar for about a hundred years. He also told stories about the good old days when the "Stars" would stop for the night on their way south. The place got its name because it was about halfway between Tijuana and Ensenada. Art told me that it was very important to meet and talk to these old timers because they carried the history of the 'real' Baja around in their heads. Art looked at me with a far off look in his eyes and said, "Remember the bartenders have the history in their heads AND the mariachi's carry the soul of Mexico in their hearts." For a long time almost everybody going south would take their time and visit with these historians. It was also a great way to have a drink and dance for a while. I was one of lucky ones because I got to know my part of Baja before the Toll Road was completed. Now, almost no one bothers to stops, relax, and listen to the stories. They just get on the Toll Road and go. They miss a bunch of great people and some wonderful stories.

Now we were heading away from the ocean, which had been our constant companion to this point. Soon we're bouncing down the old dirt road into La Mision and into the yard of the Orphanage. The kids were in class, but when they heard that old red pickup they poured out of the windows and doors. They were all over Art. He had a big grin on his face and a smile in his eyes. The kids helped with unloading and when they got to the books and school supplies you would have thought they were holding gold above their heads as they danced around the truck. The teachers cried and hugged both of us. They were truly dedicated people. Quite often they didn't even get paid.

When we finally pulled into La Salina I noticed many changes. My last visit had been six months ago. Now there was a real 'dirt' road through the flowers, and the beams of Art's house were like fingers reaching for the sky. There were several of us cops who had been conned into putting the roof on the "A" frame. Yes, we had bought 10 cases of Corona and sure we did get one extra for free. Perhaps that was why so many guys fell off the roof. We all had a ball as we worked on Art's dream. His house earned its reputation as a party house mainly because of all of the guys who were allowed to use it because they had helped to build it. When we were not working you could find us drinking warm beer, clamming for Pismo clams, or just sitting and dreaming about this wonderful place to which Art and Jack had led us. That was 1965 and I am still here looking at the ocean and drinking a beer. The only real difference is now there are a whole lot more people and the beer is COLD.

The Cantina

The CANTINA! That's all anyone calls it and everyone knows exactly what you are talking about. It's just the "Cantina" that's it

THE CANTINA
CIRCA 1965

It started out life as a simple adobe house with a kitchen, bedroom, and a living room with a great fireplace. Nothing fancy, just a bunch of windows that let in the ocean, and an uncovered patio facing the dirt road out front. There was a low wall around the patio and the still in use hitching post was just in front of the wall. Yes! The cowboys would come down off the mesa after a hard days work, tie their horses at the post, and relax in the shade of the Cantina with a shot of Tequila. *Salud* (Salute)! After a few beers you suddenly noticed that there was no bathroom. There was an outhouse located near where the horseshoe pit is now. After a few drinks on a dark night the outhouse was anything but convenient.

Bertha Kline, an American, was the original owner of the home. She had it built in 1947. We know this because as a young man Gus Arrellanes helped build the house. He says that even before it was finished it became a great party house. Bertha and Lolita Kelly would buy a couple of cases of tequila, a case of gin, and a few other things. Then they would invite people for miles around to 'drop by' and have a drink. These parties would last as long as the booze held out. I'm told that not much work was done during the week following one of these parties

Lolita Kelly lived in the large white house on the eastern edge of the lagoon. In places like Huntington Beach it would be called the 'back bay.' The street Calle Lolita is named for her.

I guess you could say that this was a pretty good start for a place that evolved into THE CANTINA. This is the only restaurant and bar in all of Baja that is known simply as "The Cantina." Think about it! All of the others have names such as, La Gloria's, Rene's, the Half Way House, Hussong's, etc.

Señor Benson bought the house in the early 60's and turned it into Rancho Benson, a small cantina. The

26

first thing he did was to have an 'indoor' bathroom installed in the area where the kitchen is now. This *cuarto de bano* was just for the women. Men still used the outhouse. It was only much later that the current men and women's restrooms were installed. It was about then that the bar doubled in size and the room where we all dance was added. The Cantina is like a living thing—it just keeps growing—the second floor "Hotel Rooms" were added in the early 80's.

Señor Benson was a very dignified Mexican man with snow-white hair. He always wore a sleeveless brown sweater over a long sleeved flannel shirt. Summer or winter, night or day, it didn't matter that was his uniform. His son "Petie" tended bar. More about him later.

A young man, Eddie, worked as a bartender, janitor, and general handyman. Early on the Cantina was only open Friday night through Sunday afternoon. No food was served. During the week the Cantina was closed but still open. No one was there to work as the bartender or anything else. The doors were unlocked and the vodka and beer were available; you just had to help yourself. As you did you were expected to 'pay the box.' The box was an old cigar box that was left behind the bar. As you drank you paid the box…Sure, It was the honor system but I never heard of anyone violating it. If you drank the last of the booze it was up to you to take all of the money and go to either Ensenada or Rosarito and buy as much vodka and beer as the money would cover. You really didn't want to take the last drink because it was a twenty-mile drive up or down the old road to either town.

The system didn't last long because Eddie was soon hired to work and live in the Cantina all week long.

What most of us might call the modern conveniences were non-existent. There was no electricity and thus no ice to cool the beer or booze. Hurricane lanterns, filled with kerosene, were scattered around the bar to provide light. Eddie complained that it took a whole day to clean the chimneys after a busy weekend. Water was trucked in and pumped to tanks on the roof. Gravity was the force that delivered the water. Oh! Yes, all of the houses had the same system until about 1984 or was it 1985?

I started coming down during the week. Eddie and I would normally be the only people in camp. He didn't speak any English at the time and I didn't speak much Spanish but we soon became very good friends. He would come down to the "A" Frame in the morning and I would fix coffee and eggs. As I worked on the house he would tell me stories about his early life and I would tell him about myself. His life was much-much more interesting than mine. As a teenager he worked for a retired Mexican Army General—that's really close to God in this part of the world. He was the General's driver and they toured all of Mexico and Latin America between 1959 and 1962. He really told some great stories. In the afternoon I would wander up to the Cantina. Eddie would go in and get us each a warm Corona (only one, never more). We would sit back with our heels over the hitching post and talk. I talked more with Eddie than any other person, except my wife, in the world. Like I said we were friends.

I'll never forget one afternoon when a real honest to God cowboy came riding down off the Mesa. We could see him as he started down then we lost him in the canyon. About a half hour later he rode up to the Cantina, tied his horse to the hitching post, and walked right by us. He was wearing Levi's, a dirty-coulda been white cowboy hat, and grimy, worn, old leather chaps. We followed him in and watched as he pulled a stool up to the bar. Acting like he owned the place, he ordered a shot of Tequila, paid and slowly sipped it. He sat ramrod straight and was definitely in no hurry to go anywhere. He ordered another and then he started to talk. The three of us talked about a big rattlesnake he had just killed on his way to the Cantina. Eddie would tell me a word in English here and there and the old guy would use an English word every now and then and of course I would understand about one word in ten. All of us used our hands quite a bit. It was a great way to spend a late afternoon. That was the only time I have seen a real, working, cowboy and his horse. No! He didn't carry a gun, but there was a .22 cal rifle tied to his saddle.

As the years went by Eddie got a lot better at understanding and speaking English and I got better at just understanding Spanish. Eddie was good looking and outgoing. He became friends with many of the *Norte Americanos*. Unfortunately, he picked up a lot of bad habits from them. The large amounts of money he was making in tips spoiled him. He began to drink heavily. Remember when he and I would only have one beer a day. He had a lot of Indian in his blood and when he got drunk he would get very-very nasty. Toward the end when he got mad at a customer he would start screaming in English and

Spanish, grab a machete and wave it over his head. Screaming at the top of his lungs he would slam it flat on the bar. Usually, the offending party would take 'one' step from the bar and be out the door. The door was fifteen feet away. Eddie would laugh, glower at the rest of the customers, and go right back to whatever he was doing. His behavior got so bad that he lost his job and ended up wandering from bar to bar in Ensenada.

I miss my friend the 'young' Eddie very much. He was a wonderful person, he always had smile on his face, and a laugh in his voice. Until the end he was a man who genuinely liked people AND was liked in return.

Before the Toll Road

In 1965 things were very different than they are today. Now you zip past Tijuana and hit the Toll Road at *Playa de Tijuana*. It's a straight shot down to La Salina. No need to stop for any reason other than the Toll Booth at Rosarito. Without stopping to pee you can make it from San Diego to the Cantina in about an hour. In '65 the same trip would take from 3 to 6 hours depending somewhat on your life style.

The first problem you would encounter was the normal 20-30 minute back up at the border. Not northbound, but going south, it was always backed up.

There were only a few lanes into Mexico and the Immigration Officers were right on the border. They stopped and checked almost every vehicle. If you were bringing anything worthwhile—like building materials—no problem! You just slipped the guy some *'mordida'* (a little bite), five or ten bucks usually handled it, no taxes or forms, and away you went.

Getting from the border involved traversing the southeastern area of downtown Tijuana with all of its crazy *gringo* drivers. Those guys never seemed to know where they were going. They were a real menace to the safe and proper flow of traffic. The traffic snarl began to thin out as you hit the *'Libre'* (the free road) as it crossed *Avenida Revolucion* and wound it's way up and over the hills toward the village of Rosarito. Soon you were rolling through the small community of La Gloria's. During the prohibition era this was the first watering hole for the Hollywood movie stars as they headed south. Leaving La Gloria's you found yourself in open farm country heading downhill toward Rosarito Beach.

The *Libre* from Tijuana all the way to Rosarito was one lane is each direction with numerous *curva peligroso* (dangerous curves). Add to this very slow moving trucks, crazy gringo's, *macho* Mexican drivers and you will understand why this strip has more little white crosses along both sides of the road than any other stretch of roadway in Baja.

31

To try and pass a slow moving truck was to take your life in your hands. This was definitely white-knuckle country.

As you dropped into the valley leading to the beach you would find a few old Indian artisans sitting by the road, selling 'real' hand carved original woodcarvings. If you wanted something special you could order it and pick it up on your next trip. There were other venders selling melons, corn, tamales, olives, and blankets. If you took your time and studied things, you would find that the prices were highest on Saturday and Sunday and much cheaper on Wednesday or Thursday. Why? Because by Wednesday the Indians were broke and on Sunday they were flush. These poor guys were truly living hand to mouth.

By the time you reached the dusty, sleepy village of Rosarito you were ready for a drink and some time to wind down after all those *curvas peligros* and those crosses of death. Remember there was no Toll Road and the main street through town, *Avenida* Juarez, was part of the *Libre* that connected Tijuana with Ensenada to the south. The City of Rosarito Beach encompassed a mere 15,000 souls half of which were North Americans. "The Hotel" was very run down and no one who knew anything bothered to stop there. If you needed gasoline this was your last chance until you hit Ensenada.

Rene's Bar and Restaurant was the last place to get a drink until you hit the Half Way House. Between Rene's and the Half Way House there was nothing but a one lane, pothole filled, road. Twenty-five miles an hour was good time.

As you approached the Half-Way House you began to notice that the 'grime' of the rat race was beginning to peel away. Most people know the story of how this place got its name but I'll tell it again just to make sure. When the Stars from Hollywood wandered down here they found that the Bar and "Motel" were halfway between T.J. and Ensenada. In those days it was a good days drive to the Half Way House and another to Ensenada. Would you believe that those glamorous people slept in those 10' by 12' rooms out back? Anyway, the Half Way House had a great dance floor and very friendly bartenders.

"I'll have a Rum and coke, No! How about a bourbon and water? No. Ok! I'll have vodka no ice. Thanks!" The drinks were somewhat limited but the people were friendly, the music was fair, and the dance floor was smooth.

Heading south you would not see another vehicle until you hit *Puerto Nuevo* (New Port) which was the home of about 75 people all of whom owed their living to the sea. Two or three of the families would invite you into their living rooms and serve you fresh lobster, beans, and rice, for so little money I won't even mention it. Señor Ortega had not yet installed refrigeration so all of the *langosta* was fresh from the sea. Cantamar was just a bump in the road. Nothing between here and La Fonda's except Campo Lopez.

Around the bend, through La Mision and, finally, home. Elapsed time 3 hours 35 minutes.

And that was rushing!

The Old Road was really the good road from the standpoint that it allowed you to stop and get to know some of the historians of Baja. Listening to them brought you much closer to the reality that the people of Baja faced in their everyday lives. In a short few words these guys could make history come alive.

When they talked about the English and Irish seamen who jumped ship along the Baja coast and married into the old families of Mexico you could picture them. Guys with white skin, blue eyes, and sometimes red flowing hair. The language must have been tough but just imagine guys who were used to boiled potatoes and other such bland things trying to get used to *salsa picante, tacos, langostos,* and *burritos.* Think of their stomachs!

They survived and prospered in this wonderful land. Look around and you will see the green or blue eyes in a dark brown face. Occasionally you will see a red head and you will know that the genes of those deserters are alive and well in Baja.

Early Construction in La Salina

The first couple of houses in La Salina were built much like when people raised barns and houses in the early days of the old west. Everyone just pitched in and a house started to rise from the ground. There were neither permits nor any real plans; they just grew out of the ground like

mushrooms. This was particularly true of the historic, "A" Frame; built by Art McLaren and his numerous friends.

The main beams were torn from an old barn in Ramona California and smuggled—how do you smuggle (40) 6"X8"X24' hunks of lumber—across the border and down to La Salina. These were followed by many more loads of free building material that went into the building of McLaren's place. This landmark grew from the soil at a cost of almost *nada* (NOTHING)!! Everyone heading south in the early days used the "A" Frame as a landmark—"once you see the "A" Frame just keep going until—." These were typical driving instructions given to newcomers to Baja from 1965 until the mid eighties. An exact copy of the A Frame can be found in *La Bufadora,* about 50 miles south of the original. It seems that the guy who built it liked the "A"frame so much that he copied it exactly.

The guys who worked on the A-Frame were cops who worked for Captain McLaren in San Diego. We all worked our butts off for the "old man." Sometimes there would only be two or three of us and other times there would be a dozen. But, always we would have at least 10 cases+one of Corona to keep us working. In those days Corona was known as "skunk beer" because, sometimes, it smelled so bad that you had to hold your nose to drink it. *Es Verdad*, (it's true) they brought the beer to Baja via train from the mainland. If the train broke down in the desert, as it so often did, the heat did weird things to the beer.

Art always barbecued chicken halves; they ended up being well seasoned with sand before they were ready to eat. The only meal he provided, assuming you worked all day, was that chicken ala sand and Mexican rolls covered

36

with butter and garlic.   That was it!   If you wanted breakfast or lunch you had to bring your own.   The Cantina (Rancho Benson's) did not serve food.

The day we put the roof on the old house, it was old even as it was being built, was a time none of us will ever forget.   Day one found six of us nailing on the 1"x6"x8's that covered the roof.   It was a scorcher of day in the summer of '65 and we were left with nothing to drink by about 4 o'clock.   Sure, Art cooked the crummy chicken but we had nothing with which to wash it down.   We called it quits and headed for the Cantina for a few cool ones.   In those days no one would be caught dead drinking the water in Baja.   We all 'knew' that it was *no seguro* (unsafe).   Well, we did all right by the Cantina until they ran out of booze.   This lack of refreshments occurred at about 8 o'clock as close as I can remember.   We closed the place and wandered, splashing, across the lagoon—now the Marina—to Dick Eckert's trailers in Angel's Camp.   Dick hauled his trailers into Angel's in 1958 and that makes him the most senior gringo around La Salina.   When we got to Dick's trailers we found he had neglected to drink a whole half-gallon of rum.   We rapidly corrected that oversight and the rum was gone before we 'retired' for the <u>evening</u>!

Five o'clock came terribly early but we were all young so we all trouped back across the lagoon and started working on the roof about the time the sun came up.   Right! No breakfast, but we were all full of the night before.   You talk about a kick; the roof of the A-Frame is 24 feet high. Art had (2) six-foot ladders, a four footer, and (1) eight footer.   Ernie Trumper and I laid the ladders' one atop of the other and they almost reached the peak of the roof. We both did very well hauling the 90-pound rolls of roofing to the top where we would nail it down and let it roll down the roof. Someone would cut it off at the bottom. This continued, up and down, up and down until the roof was finished. You should know that Art and a couple of other guys made it halfway up the rickety ladders before they fell and rolled down onto the sand below. Ernie and I stayed on top and laughed our "A's" off. All in all it was a great weekend. Art got his roof finished for ten cases of *cerveza* and some rubbery chicken. We all shared an experience that none of us will ever forget. It caused a couple of us to return to Baja year after year after year after year...

A few weeks later my son, Bernie, and I came down by ourselves. Our task for the weekend was to frame in the kitchen and paper it so that Cayo and Gus could plaster it the following week. Bernie was only 7 years old and he really didn't do a whole lot of work. He ran back and forth to the beach while I framed in the kitchen. We had a cold dinner and were in our sleeping bags by 8 o'clock. It seemed like only a few minutes later that he was hollering, "Wake up dad it's time to go back to work." WOW!! The moon had come up and it was so bright he thought it was daylight. I looked at my watch and it was only 10 o'clock. "Go back to sleep kid!"

If you look closely at the window at the, upper, south end of the house you will see that it is cracked. This happened when young Bernie stepped on it as he chased rabbits through the bushes around the house. He played hard that day. He was up and down the dunes and out into the surf. He found a friend, *Ricardo*, and they wandered around the camp looking for old Indian arrowheads. They found a few and *Ricardo* let him keep all of them because he had *un million* at home. Ricardo is the oldest son of my *comparde* (more than a friend) Cayo. On the way home all he could talk about was what a great guy Ricardo was and how he was going to share his arrowheads with the kids at school. So now you see another important side of early camp life!

A Little Water Goes A Long Way!

When I first came to La Salina no one really even thought about water. We certainly didn't drink it! A couple of gallons would last two guys a whole weekend. After all, the only thing you did with it was brush your teeth and wash your face. Oh! Sure, a few people used a little more because they drank coffee in the morning.

As women began coming into camp the need for water more than doubled. A couple would require five gallons of the precious stuff to see them through a weekend. At this point "all" of the water used in camp came from north of the border and no one wasted that which had to be hauled so far. Vodka and beer could be purchased a lot easier in Rosarito Beach or Ensenada and they "were" much safer to drink than the local water.

I knew a couple of fishermen who NEVER EVER brought water into camp. One of the reasons that they moved further south was because so many people started using water with an ever-greater frequency.

About two years after the camp was first established a guy named Heine (he had a trailer at the north end of camp) decided to build the first INDOOR bathroom that would also have a shower. None of us really believed that this was his idea. He 'was' one of the guys! We all knew that his wife, Dottie, was the driving force behind this ruination of our previously simple camp life.

Anyway, he did it! He built a two-story block building with a 200-gallon water tank inside the top. The plan was to have water pumped up to the storage tank and then gravity fed to the shower, sink, and toilet. Fine, a great idea, but outhouses were a whole lot simpler. All you needed to do was to dig a hole, throw some lime in and build a little wooden  shack to provide a little privacy and to keep the wind and sand out. Now Heine had so complicated life that he also had to build a septic tank to hold all of the 'stuff' that came out of the "shower tower." Prior to this if a fool wanted to get clean he could either go jump in the ocean or drive down the old road to the public baths in Ensenada.

The only guys who were willing to drive to town were the single ones who would then hit the bars and end up in a house with a "red light" affixed next to the front door.

Soon Peggy got Larry to build their house with the "first" indoor plumbing in La Salina. It should be noted that Peggy was the sister of that original troublemaker, Dottie. Keeping up with the Jones had come to paradise.

Now all of the houses (7) and a few trailers all had some form of above ground water storage. We didn't get electricity until much later so everybody had to rely upon gravity to deliver more and more water.

In the beginning we only needed two gallons of water for a weekend and now we had 50, 500, and even one 1,000-gallon water tanks all over the place. Some were white, some yellow and the biggest one, at Harold and Peggy Reagles *casita,* had a great Smiley Face painted on each ends.

It should be noted that all of this water did not reduce the consumption of alcohol in camp by even one drop!!

Well, guess what! With all of this progress someone looked around and realized that they did not have a water source in camp. So things got even more complicated. Now the movers and shakers-Art, Larry, and

Heine started hitting everyone up for money so the camp could buy Cayo a water truck.

He could then haul the water from La Mision valley to fill the water tanks. Soon Cayo was the proud owner of a beat up old truck with a leaky 800-gallon water tank and a small gasoline pump.

This era was known as the first stage of creeping progress in Paradise!

Shortly after we got electricity service in camp people began to build under ground *pillas* (water storage), the above water tanks were so unsightly don't you know, and the standard size became 1,000 gallons based upon Cayo's water truck holding 800 gallons. Things slowed down and everyone went back to enjoying life until his water truck broke down and we had to pony up more money to get a 'newer' truck. This one came with a 1,000-gallon tank. This caused a re-thinking of what the standard size of a pilla should be. The shakers and movers decreed that 1,500 to 2,000 gallon *pilla* would be perfect. This would allow us to order water when we still had <u>500 gallons</u> in the ground.

So, again, my friends you can see how we started out using <u>two gallons</u> a weekend and now we "worried" when we "only" have 500 gallons in storage. That is truly progress with a capital "P"—I really wonder!

Oh! Yes, the original "shower tower" still exists and is still in use. It should be designated as La Salina Historical Marker # 2.

Party Time

Parties between 1960 and 1965 were basically men only. There were no houses in La Salina del Mar and the only people who frequented Benson's were fishermen or surfers who camped on the beach. They did a lot of drinking but without the partying. When McLaren's House became habitable and a few trailers were moved into camp women began to show up in ever-greater numbers. Now the parties changed from 'work parties' to the real thing.

The first fiesta in camp was held on the sand at McLaren's. The Mariachi Band arrived on a Friday at about 4 o'clock. Liquid refreshments consisted of wine, rum, vodka, and beer and they all flowed rather freely. The dinner featured Art's famous barbecued chicken halves, tossed garlic salad, and Mexican rolls. The band played all night and people from all over the mesa showed up to eat, drink, and try to dance in the sand.

The Mariachi's ate and drank right along with the rest of us so it was not surprising that as the night progressed first one then another member of the group would drop out and crash in the sand. After a while the first one would arise and begin to play again. This went on  in relays for the whole weekend. We always had music it just sounded different depending on which guy was resting. Remember what Art said about the Mariachi's carrying the soul of Mexico around in their hearts. Well, they played all of those emotions out for us during that wonderful weekend.

Early Saturday morning several of the guys went to Ensenada to buy dinner for the day. One giant green sea turtle—it WAS legal to hunt and sell them in those days. In fact, most of the old timers had large sea turtle shells on the walls of their houses. It was a wonderful day with lots of sun, fun, music, and friends. Not to mention the beer that flowed freely all day. We dug a huge pit in the sand and started a fire that burned for several hours until the coals were just right. To cook the turtle it was placed, still in the shell, at an angle over the coals. The cook basted it several times, first with vodka, and then with wine. Most of us thought this was an incredible waste of good booze! Dinner was fabulous! Turtle, beans, rice and tortillas. We all ate until we couldn't eat anymore.

Yes! It was legal to eat turtle in those good old days. The Mariachi's continued to play, eat, drink, and sleep. Over the weekend there must have been at least a hundred people show up for the party. Some now and some later. Everyone who attended that bash will always remember it. Sunday started out real slow with not much movement around camp until about noon. We still had some sea turtle and people began to organize—throw together—a potluck! We were down to a six-pack of Corona when someone found a couple of large bottles of La Palmas Rum. The Mariachi's had stopped playing and were sleeping in the shade. At about 3 o'clock a fight broke out between a family of free loaders from Angel's Camp and the good guys from La Salina. It turned out to be quite a good fight. The family from Angel's never did return to this part of Baja.

On many occasions what started out to be a clam raking adventure turned into a great party when it was found that enough clams had been harvested to feed everyone in camp. The call would go out, 'lets have a party.' One person would make chowder; another would do a clam cocktail. The next gal would throw together a salad. A guy would bring some baked beans and before you knew it a feast awaited. If someone didn't have any food they were sure to have some booze. The really important individual was the one who brought the ice cubes. These impromptu party's were the best. Later in the evening someone would bring out a guitar—once a guy pulled out a Jews-harp and had us all singing along.

As the camp became more developed the women started planning things like the 4th of July beach party. These events would last from about noon until after dark.

One guy had a school yellow Baja Bug and he was kept busy ferrying the ladies back and forth to the restrooms. It was at one of these events that Jack Speer was actually seen to eat food!!!. Most people had never seen Jack partake of anything other than liquid refreshments.

These party's were the thing that bound our camp together and formed its character!

Party time anyone?

Indian Petroglyphs

Shortly after the "A" Frame was finished Larry and Peggy Pearson wandered into camp. Like so many of the *Pioneros* (pioneers) they had known Jack Speer, the founder of La Salina, in Downey California. They wandered around camp for a while before they picked out a lot just north of the 'A' Frame. They wrote Jack a check for the $200.00 down payment and the second lot in La Salina was sold.

A few weeks later they pulled an old trailer into camp and plunked it down. Soon, construction was started on the second house to be built in camp. They hired Gus Arrellanes and Cayo to build them a beautiful blockhouse with a Mexican tile roof. This was the first house that complied with the Corporations' guidelines that all houses MUST be built of fireproof materials. Art's had been built of all wood and was very combustible. Remember that the closest *Bombadeo* (fire truck) was over an hour away.

Larry had suffered a massive heart attack and his doctor had told him that he only had a very short time to live. This prompted him to move to Mexico where the stress of modern life was nearly non-existent. Larry reminded me a lot of the comedian W.C. Fields. He had such large, sad, eyes and a wide mouth that always seemed about to break out in laughter even though his eyes failed to follow. Larry prospered with the leisurely new style of Baja and he lived for several more, fishing filled, years.

It was a hoot watching Cayo and Gus pull the roof of an old car up to a construction site to mix concrete. The next things that arrived were several loads of volcanic rock; which was used as a sub footing. When I asked them why they were building a 'sub footing.' They explained, mainly with hand motions and demonstrations, that the sub footing was necessary because of the porous sandy soil. They used volcanic rock because there was a lot of it around and it was cheap! They showed me how the air holes in the rock made the cement they pored over it bind together extremely well. All of the footings were dug by hand with the excess dirt being hauled away in an old wheelbarrow. That out of round steel wheel squeak could be heard throughout the camp. Next came blocks, blocks, and more blocks. These were followed by numerous bags of Mexican concrete in 50 *kilo* (110 pounds) bags. These relatively small people, 5'6" to 5'9" and 135 pounds, would lift those 110-pound bags all day long while the larger North Americans would complain about lifting 96-pound (American) bags.

It was truly incredible to watch those guys go about building a modern house. They had NO cement mixers and water had to be hauled into camp in 55 gallon drums. Working with almost NO tools it was just amazing to see the beautiful homes they concocted from rock, sand, cement, block and sweat. I got in their way all of the time and they were both very patient with me as they answered my many questions. I learned all kinds of Mexican words that are of almost no use unless you are constructing a house in Mexico. How do you work a word like *nivel* (level) into day-to-day conservation?

Peggy and Larry had the real spirit of Baja. One day you would see them watching the construction of their home and the next you would see them leaving camp in Larry's old jeep. It was crazy, here was a guy who was supposed to die any minute and he was heading off to the wilds of old Baja. They would load his jeep with, 5 gallons of water, 15 gallons of extra gas, a couple of gallons of rum, a few staples, a compass, and his fishing poles. With that he and Peggy would wander into the interior of Baja for days at a time. This was in 1966 when only the very brave ventured south of Ensenada. No road maps-almost no roads-just a compass.

They would always return with Indian Arrowheads and stories of Indian Petroglyphs found in out of the way

48

caves. These two were genuine additions to the history of La Salina. Larry was friendly and open and Peggy was harsh and caustic. He was always ready to help and she was ready to put you in your place.

Larry lived here for a few more years and then Peggy became the first widow in La Salina. She lived here for 27 years. The lease on her ocean front lot cost her a grand $25.00 per month. Yep! $200.00 down and $25.00 per month for 30 years was the going rate in the early years.

After every heavy windstorm you would find Peggy wandering around camp, harvesting the Indian Arrowheads that had been uncovered by the shifting sands. For several years Peggy would point to a large 'hump' in the road, that leads to the beach and tell anyone who would listen that someday she would dig it up. She would always say, "I'll bet you it's a big, old, *Matate.*" Finally, after a real howler she dug down a few inches and pulled out a great big Indian *Matate* (a large porous bowl like rock) that was used by the Indians to grind corn or acorns. She took this find to the Natural History Museum in San Diego for dating. They told her that it was about 2,000 years old. They also looked at her collection of old arrowheads and said they came from the same general period.

So! I guess you could say, that in spite of the fact that we see ourselves as *pioneros*, we are really all 'new comers' to La Salina.

The Sea Captain of La Salina

Now I would like to introduce you to the most dapper, outgoing, man I have ever met. David Pringle!!  When he came to La Salina I do not know. That Fifi was with him everyone knows. He always wore a silk scarf at his neck and a Greek Fishermen's cap upon his head. He was extremely careful about his attire and his person. Her reminded me of the famous English Actor David Nevin. He had a quiet, slow, smile and carried himself true and straight. He acted like he was the Mayor of La Salina. He took all newcomers in camp under his wing and took great pleasure in conducting a tour of the camp.

He would invariable meet me, shortly after I arrived at the Cantina. I would buy him a drink and he would give me my first Spanish lesson of the day. He insisted that I learn at least <u>one</u> Spanish word for each day I was in camp.

The first words he taught me were—*Disfrutar de vida* (enjoy life). He proved himself to be every inch a gentleman. It should be pointed out that this fact did not, ever, cause him to stoop to buying anyone else a drink. Drinks were that which he received and not what he gave.

He told everyone that he was a licensed Captain of the Fishing Boats. No one ever asked him which boats or what country. His personality was such that you just did not ask such demeaning questions. He had that smile and a certain the flair that prohibited us gringo's from asking any really meaningful questions. David could talk for hours, even longer, if someone else was buying the drinks. He knew everything that was worth knowing about this area of Baja. I often wish he were still around to use as a source for this book.

He was a solid friend of Jack Speers and as such was well received by all who came into camp. It seems that Jack, David, and Bobby Placier, the Marshall of Ensenada, were doing what they did most of the time—drinking. On this particular day it was at Hussongs Cantina in Ensenada. They had been drinking with the likes of Fred Hoctor and Phil Harris. Fred was to become the author of a wonderful book—Baja Haha and Phil was a well known comedian and TV celebrity—Suddenly a very big, and very drunk, Mexican guy took exception to something Bobby said or did. They exchanged a few heated words and suddenly the guy pulled a knife and tried to kill Bobby. David interceded, ala David Nevin, disarmed the big guy, and apparently saved Bobby's life.

As a result Bobby asked Jack to look after David for the rest of his life. Jack kept his word and as a consequence our Sea Captain led a charmed life.

We knew that David had no meaningful source of income and his house (trailer) was not hooked up to electricity. We knew that he had never bought a tank of propane. He did, however, always have heat and lights in the casita that he and Fifi shared.

We all wondered about this but never asked because of his standing with Jack. David was such a warm and wonderful guy that everyone tried to ignore his unspoken shortcomings. We all were happy to have him around. He was just plain fun to be around. We did to start locking our propane tanks together so that they could not wander off during the night.

It was a sad day when the police came to Captain David's place and took David to the Ensenada Police Department. Jack was true to his word and managed to get David released and he soon returned to camp. No one exhibited any desire to inquire as to why the *Polica* had detained our Sea Captain. After this incident occurred David became a mere shadow of himself. His shoulders slumped; his smile and flair were gone. He lacked the vitality that had characterized his previous flamboyant approach to life. He died soon after. I think of David often. He was one of those men who brighten others lives as he touched them in passing. This was definitely true of his wanderings through my early life in this *little bit of paradise* that is La Salina.

I honestly believe that you would all be enriched should you be allowed the privilege of someday meeting a Captain David.

Disfrutar de Vida!

Putty Putty
A Cement Mixer for Cayo

Up until late 1968 all of the construction in La Salina and in most of Baja was done by mixing all of the cement and plaster by hand in the roof of some old junked car. The roof was cut off and all material was removed; then it was turned upside down and it formed a perfect, and cheap, large bowl like container. It was great for mixing cement and it could be easily dragged from one construction side to the next. If any real distance was involved it was just tossed it into the back of a pickup for transportation. This worked wonderfully for the first 6 or 7 houses in camp. Then the shakers and movers decided that they should put the bite on everyone and buy a used, gasoline driven, cement mixer for Cayo to insure that the cement was 'properly' mixed.

Art McLaren was selected—he was the only one foolish enough to offer—to find, buy, and transport a putty-putty mixer to La Salina. Finding the mixer was no *problemo*, but getting it back to camp proved to be a large problem, even for Art. He realized that he would be unable to get the necessary paperwork to move such a 'modern machine' into Mexico. There were and still are laws to protect the laboring man in Mexico.

Art thought about this problem for quite a while. He came up with a great ploy to get by Mexican Customs at the border. He hooked the mixer up to his old Ford pickup, loaded the truck with shovels, picks and other tools of the trade and headed for the border. This was on a Friday and he timed it so he would hit the border at about noon. He had already decided that his story would be that he had finished work early and that he was just going to Tijuana to get a haircut.

When he got to the border an alert guard noticed that he was pulling a big bright orange cement mixer. The *Inmigracion Officer* stopped him and asked him what he thought he was doing bringing this fancy modern machine into Mexico. Art (the fox) told him that he was just going to get a haircut in TJ and would return to the U.S. in a few minutes. Art even had cement on his hands, which he waved in the face of the Officer to prove that his story was true. He kept telling his story in English and the guard kept telling him to turn around and leave his mixer in San Ysidro and come back without it if he really wanted to get a haircut. Perhaps the reason the customs guy didn't believe his story was because Art was almost completely bald.

Anyway, he turned Art around and sent him back to the States. Mac made a U-turn and went back across the border only to find the same guard; who again, in Spanish, ordered him back north across the border. Art argued as hard as he could, in English, for the right to get his haircut. This went on a total of seven (7) trips until the guard laughed and, in English, asked Art how long he was willing to drive around in circles. Art replied, also laughing, *"Los total Dia mi Amigo y toda la noche"* (all day and all night). The guard waved his arm and declared, *"Pase, Pase mi gringo amigo"* (go ahead, go ahead, my friend).

Art arrived in La Salina with the first cement mixer, with a motor, in the history of Baja. It only took him 6 ½ hours total time from San Diego.

It was great! Now all of us gringo's knew that in the future we would get well mixed, strong, cement; and the working guys could lean on their shovels and watch the cement mix itself.

The mixer still sets in Cayo's yard along with all of his other treasurers. It no longer has a carburetor, but it runs just as well with a can of gas suspended above the motor so that gravity can feed the necessary gasoline.

Conversations with Eddie

Coming to La Salina as I did during the week allowed us to really communicate with each other. Eddie's English was very broken and he often had to search for an acceptable word to convey his meaning. I on the other hand had almost no knowledge of the Spanish language. In spite of these drawbacks we got along wonderfully. We both did a lot of gesturing, sometimes we even got down on the ground and drew pictures, but communicate we did, probable much better than most *Norte Americano*s. Being the only people around somehow made each of us very important in the others eyes. We cared about each other and we were truly interested in each other's cultures... It helped tremendously that we were in no hurry and that there was no outside interference from other people.

We could count on someone dropping by the Cantina, perhaps, once a month during the week and they were normally lost gringo's who just wanted directions to the nearest Gas Station. It always amazed to me that anyone would drive down from Los Angeles, cross the border into a foreign country, and never even think of filling up their car before heading south. I guess they expected to find a service station on every corner like you would in the U.S. Not down here, you got gas in Tijuana, Rosarito Beach, or Ensenada. Nothing in between. Eddie always laughed, in a good-natured way, when the people panicked because their gas gauge read empty and they were more than 30 miles from the nearest service station. We let them dangle for a few minutes and then one of us would walk around back and return with a five-gallon can of gasoline. People were always more than happy to pay Eddie $10.00 U.S. for the gas. That was one of the ways he made his meager pay stretch from one month to the next.

Eddie told me that he was half Indian and that made him a *mestizo* (half-caste). I told him I was half Irish and half Dutch with a little French thrown in for luck. He laughed and told me that it was not the same thing. That was when I learned that growing up as a *mestizo* in Mexico made you a second class citizen and kept you from getting some of the better jobs. (This has changed in the past few years but it can still be a block in moving from one social class to another). Eddie was a very smart individual and it made him very angry that he was limited to working in a Cantina for the rest of his life.

He had a young wife and a couple of kids in Ensenada but he almost never talked about them and he never brought them into camp. His private life was exactly that, "private." His attitude in this reflected that of most Mexican men. You could become friends with them but it was fairly rare for a gringo to become friends with their families.

If you were allowed to meet the family it usually meant that you had really become accepted and you would end up being a 'part of the family'. I am particularly proud that I have that kind of relationship with *Cayo,* his wife *Julia* (pronounced Hulia), and their kids—Flora, Joe, Ricardo, Martha, and Raul. If I need anything and they have it—it's mine. If they need something I will try to get it for them.

My relationship with Eddie allowed me to learn much and understand a little more of the proud culture of people of Baja California.

Via Con Dios mi Amigo!!

A Little Bit of This And
A Little Bit of That

Here are a bunch of little things that may give you a better taste for the flavor of early life in La Salina del Mar.

Oso Negro Vodka came in Gallon jugs only—at least that is what we all thought for years. At $3.95 a bottle it was the cheapest booze around. It also had a good kick. The glass bottle came with a Black Bear on a key chain. A couple of the early houses had privacy screens 10 feet high by 10 feet wide entirely made of "*Oso Negro*" key chains. The bottles were great for storing kerosene. You took an empty bottle to a Mercado and filled it with *'kerosen.'* You would find a faucet somewhere on the back wall of the store. There were no signs you just knew that you could fill your bottle by just opening the faucet—sure! Put the bottle under it first. It usually cost about 15 cents for a gallon and this usually kept the Hurricane Lanterns going for a month or two. You had to make sure not to confuse the bottles because kerosene was a real no-no to drink!

Las Palmas Rum bottles—one-gallon size—came encased around the bottom with a real woven straw basket. They were very decorative as candleholders. The rum was good but not quite as cheap as the Oso Negro vodka. You never used the Las Palmas bottles to store kerosene because it was almost the same color as the rum! It's funny but when they replaced the straw basket with a 'plastic' one people quit buying the stuff. Artistic?—Who knows!

In the late 1960's it was not unusual for a guy named 'Blackie' to land his airplane on the unfinished Toll Road and taxi it up to the Cantina. He would stop the plane just in front of the old hitching post, shut her down, and wander in and have a few drinks before he heading south to San Quintin to go fishing. I don't know what kind of a plane it was but it had a high wing, extra large tires, and was painted blue and yellow. Once the Toll Road was opened he quit dropping in for a drink.

Perhaps you've noticed the Airplane Propeller mounted on the wall in the Cantina. If you did you also noticed that both tips of the 'prop' were badly bent. This was from the plane of another guy, his name is lost to history, who used to land and take off from the beach in front of the Cantina. His plane also had a high, wide wing, an open cockpit, and was painted a dull rusty red. It had large wide tires for sand landings.

He used to spend the afternoons drinking and if he found an attractive looking woman who wanted to "go hide in the clouds" he would load her in his plane and roar off into the blue. Once, on landing he bent the propeller when his plane nosed over on hitting a soft patch of sand. Undaunted, he hired a young Mexican kid to baby sit his wounded plane and took off, in a bus, for San Diego to get a 'new prop'. He came back on Monday, replaced the propeller and took off. We never saw him again but he did leave the 'bent prop' for us to remember him by.

Early on, one of the ways we would while away a quiet morning was by attempting to make an "old Servel Gas Refrigerator" work. It usually turned out that a 'gas spider' had built a nest in the gas orifice in such a manner as to stop the flow of the propane. These Servels were a throwback to the 1930-40's and were used all over the States where electricity was not available. Most of them found their way into Mexico and some are still in use where electric juice is still not to be had. Getting one of these to run again normally involved a tire pump, some thin wire, a brush, a lot of beer, and a few camp 'experts.' I never could understand how you could use propane and heat to make something get "cold." If you find one in running order grab it—they are now worth six to eight hundred dollars apiece.

One of the ladies in camp looking for a propane gas leak with a cigarette lighter. Definitely not smart.

June 1981 electricity came to camp. Most people were happy because now they could do away with those 'unsightly' gravity flow water tanks. There was a problem when the electricity went out and you couldn't pump your water out of the pilla and into your toilet! You could always depend on gravity!!

With the advent of electricity the management at the Cantina encountered a major problem. David, Ramon, and all of bartenders refused to use a "blender" to mix drinks. They had learned how to make the "Best Margaritas in

Baja" by *Agitar de Lata* or shake the can. Just picture it, first the ice, then the lime, the mix and a generous pour of Tequila. Now put the lid on the can AND shake it over the right shoulder, then next to the left ear, up and down from right to left, then slowly (as if listening to it) next to the right ear—then slowly, ever so slowly pour it into a glass with the rim encrusted with salt. An art form suddenly threatened by electricity; a ritual of the ages gone in the name of progress. Mixed in the blender it became frothy—more feminine—it had no soul! You people don't even know that you are drinking an inferior product. Ramon knows and secretly in his Mexican heart he hates it!!

It was crazy, but up until the mid to late 80's Ramon or David would knock on your door and ask if they could 'borrow' a bottle. Whatever you had. Vodka-why not, bourbon-ok, tequila-fine, rum-sure! They would borrow, for the Cantina, whatever you had to lend. The nutty thing was that you would then wander up to the Cantina and 'buy' a few drinks.

Does that make sense? Not really, but you forgot the fellowship of drinking with your friends---or friends that you might meet. Forget the fact that you were paying four (or was it six) times the original cost of 'your' booze.

Who knows, they may even return the bottle next week—but don't count on it. Just enjoy the feeling of the weight of civilization flowing away and leaving a little *"tranquilidad"* in your heart and your very being.

Oh! Yea! Way back, so the story goes, in the late 1930's and early 40's a Japanese farmer raised strawberries

62

in La Salina. All of the Mexicans 'knew' that he was a spy because they saw him watching all of the ships going by. To this day, if you talk to some of the real old timers, they will swear that he was a spy. They will also tell you that an "American Artillery Unit," complete with searchlights, was stationed on the cliffs around what is now Baja Mar Golf Course.

Streetlights came to our camp in 1985. Lu Ann Swaim was the main force behind this "progress." I fought tooth and nail but to no avail. We lost the moon and the stars and we can no longer see the phosphorescence in the crown of the waves as they surge against the shore under the light of the wonderful Mexican Moon. Sure, security is enhanced but at what cost! What have we lost and what have we gained?

NADA, it is such a small word only four letters, but if you say it with meaning it will open the hearts of most Mexicans—it means "thank you" or "it is nothing"—it is best used when someone thanks you for something—to respond with "*de Nada*" releases the receiver of any sense of owing. That is a wonderful thing to do, say, and mean. de Nada—it rolls so smoothly off the tongue.

Crossing the border and feeling all of your burdens falling away. Replaced by an inner peace that seems impossible to attain in the States.

Meeting a total stranger while walking on the beach and after a few minutes of conversation feeling like you have been friends for years.

Barney Karger, the President of the Corporation, telling David Medina, the manager of the Cantina, that he insisted upon 'receipts' for all of the *Mordida* (a little bite) he paid to people in Enseneda. Believe it! He wanted them to sign for the bribes they were taking. David almost went nuts over that one.

The three musketeers wandering down the main drag shortly after dark. When asked why they were calling it a night so early, Darlene, stumbling into a soft shoe, replied, "Boy, what a boring, I mean really boring Saturday night at the Cantina." To which Bill replied, "Sure, right, no wonder you're bored, It's SUNDAY." Linda broke up laughing and muttered something about, "What an Idiot."

Operation Intercept

Early on in the 1970's Lu Ann and I were sitting around the house trying to decide what we would do with our one-week of vacation. We didn't have a whole lot of money so we had just planned to hang out. I picked up the morning paper and noticed that the U.S. Federal Government had instituted a new program at the border, "Operation Intercept," which had gone into effect two days before. This was a new program to reduce the number of 'illegal aliens' crossing into the United States at the world's busiest border at Tijuana/San Diego. Typically, our Government had not bothered to contact their counterparts in Mexico City. This caused a rapid, typical, and drastic reaction by the Mexican bureaucrats.

The Mexicans countered with a program where they were threatening to inoculate; Yes! with a needle, any *gringo* who crossed the border into Mexico. As I read the story to Lu Ann we both began to smile.

We packed our old 1966 Dodge Van with our sleeping bags, water, a six pack of Safeway Brown Derby beer, a few Dr Peppers, some instant coffee and we were off for Beautiful Baja.

We realized that the Mexicans Immigration Officers would not shoot us (inoculate) and that we would likely have most of Baja to ourselves. When we got to the border there were no cars in front of us. We just waved and zoomed across the border.

We took the *Libre* road and as we climbed the hills past all of those white little crosses we were delighted to find that we had obviously guessed right. There were no gringo cars in Baja. We cruised past Rosarito Beach in record time. Our first stop was at 'Raul's' Restaurant, which is just north of *Puerto Nuevo*. We wandered in and found the place deserted. Looking around we found Yolanda back in the *cocina* cooking some *pulpo*. She was one of the owners of the place and she was definitely not happy with 'those guys in Mexico City.' She told us that the threat of inoculations had totally killed her business and that we were her first customers in two days.

We had a Corona and a coke as we chatted with her. We had known Yolanda for about five years, but in the normal course of business we had never gotten to know her background. The lack of business allowed the three of us to relax and get to know each other better. We were surprised to find that Yolanda and her brother had gone to Grammar School, in Los Angeles, with Lu Ann. Raul, her dad, was a Mexican but the rest of the families were Americans.

Yolanda asked us if we would like some of the octopus that she was cooking. I said, "Sure, Great!" Lu just stuck her nose up in the air.

Yolanda laughed and brought us a plate full of fried *pulpo with limes*. It was very tasty even as it was a bit chewy. She told us how she had gone diving down by the cliffs at the rear of the Restaurant and how she had caught the octopus by putting her arm into small caves at the base of the cliffs. The octopus latched onto her arm and that is how 'she caught it'. We had a few more beers, said our good byes and headed south on the 'old road.' Wonderful, no traffic! We did have Baja to ourselves! Pulling into La Salina we found that the only people in camp were the Reagles. Peggy invited us in for a drink. The road had been very dusty so were only too happy to accept. They told us that Larry and Peggy Pearson had just left camp because they wanted to go fishing further south. They also had realized that the 'inoculation bit' would discourage tourists from visiting. Larry knew that they would have the road to themselves all the way to *Bahia de Los Angeles*. The Cantina was closed so we wandered down to the beach and spend a few hours all alone just playing like a couple of kids. I tried to talk Lu into skinny-dipping to which she relied, "No way Jose! You gotta be out of your mind." We spent the night at the "A" Frame. The quiet was so loud that it was unreal.

Up early the next morning, we had coffee, peanut butter sandwiches, and we were off. We went back to *La Mision* and picked up the winding, hilly, Old Road. We took our time and visited villages that we had not even noticed before. We wandered down the hills and through *Canon de Tigre* (Canyon of the Tiger). The old timers swear that many years ago a sheepherder had found the remains of a Saber Tooth tiger; after a big flood had uncovered the tigers resting place on the side of the canyon.

Soon we were approaching *El Sauzal*. You always knew when you got within a couple of miles of this small fishing village. The smell was always horrendous! The only business in town was a Fish Cannery. Up with the windows until you hit the outskirts of Ensenada.

We stopped at Hussong's Cantina and found the bartender talking to himself. The place is <u>never</u> empty—but it was until we entered. Hussong's is without a doubt the best-known bar in all three of the California's. You could've fired a cannon down *Avenida Lopez Mateos* (the main drag) and not hit even a seagull. Next we visited *Café El Rey Sol* (Eye of The Sun) for a late lunch. A family who had emigrated from Argentina established El Rey's in the 1890's. This is one of the finest French-Mexican restaurants anywhere. Not only is the food outstanding but their pastry cart is supreme. Our neighbors in the States had dinner here one time on our recommendation and left town broke! They both love sweets and could not resist the pastry cart. Thinking that desert came with the meal they had one of each kind of pastry on the cart! The pastries are expensive- and- they do not come with the meal!

Heading south on the Trans Peninsular Highway (mostly a one lane road in each direction south of Ensenada) we came upon the olive stands just south of town. I never can resist so we stopped and bought a couple of bottles (recycled-all sizes and shapes) of home cured green olives. We'll stop here on the way back for some corn on the cob with chili powder. The corn is always tough but tasty.

We'll be turning off the Highway a little before we hit the farming community of *Maneadero*. This tiny village is the true jumping off spot in Baja. Here you <u>must</u> display the proper papers or you may not proceed any further south. Should your papers include pictures of the various American Presidents then the other more official papers could be waved and you were on your way!

We headed west to *Punta Banda and La Bufadora* (the blow hole). Winding up the hills toward the point, we pulled off the road at Three Sisters Rock, and set up camp for the night. We made our camp at a spot at the edge of a cliff overlooking the entire south end of *Bahia Todo Santos* (All Saints Bay). We were all alone! No one for miles. We passed the last house about 5 miles back and there was nothing and no one until we got to the blowhole.

Quiet, quiet, deafening quiet. We watched the small boats scurrying back to their nests on the eastern edge of the bay just as night fell.

"Bam, Bam, Bang!" I'm awake in an instant. Who is shooting a shotgun and at whom are they shooting? I grab a flashlight and creep out of the van to see if I can tell what is going on. It's about 5 o'clock and the only lights I can see are far off in Ensenada. Man it is really dark and I mean dark. No electricity and no lights. Nothing! Back to bed, but no more sleep that night.

Up at first light and still no clue as to the shotgun blasts.

As we drank our coffee we were visited by dozens of Brown Pelicans flying over us in formation. Their wingspans are as wide as I am tall! And I'm over 6 foot. Using the updraft created by the cliff they sail above, just skimming over our heads. Nothing else, just us and the Pelicans. *Magnifico!* (Magnificent)

We arrived at the La Bufadora at about 10 o'clock and found that it was low tide so the waves will not be forcing the water spouts through the rocks. We'll miss it but the Pelicans were worth the whole trip. We ordered a couple of fish tacos for breakfast. Interesting, all of the trash and leftover food was tossed directly out a window and down into the gorge below. No wonder the place is overrun by sea gulls. And it stinks!

Talking with the guy who fixed our tacos gave us an explanation for the shotgun blasts in the night. It seems that the dolphins enjoy playing at the base of the cliff.

After they leap out of the water they 'splat' back into the waves and it sounds just like a shotgun blast. You would be right if you say that the dolphins scared the hell out of us.

Heading back to the States we both gave thanks to bureaucrats in both the United States and Mexico. Without knowing it they had arranged for us to have this wonderful trip all to ourselves.

A once in a lifetime trip even for Baja!

Conchita the Cook

When the Cantina opened for business in late 1963 it was called Rancho Benson's and was only open Friday through Sunday afternoon. The only thing you could buy was booze and that was it!

In 1970 Jack Speer got an idea to expand the service and add a food menu. Early in 1971 he found a cook who was willing to work in La Salina. Remember it was in the middle of nowhere in those days. Conchita lived in Tijuana and refused to ride the bus. She didn't know how to drive and she didn't have a car anyway. So she had to be picked up every Friday morning and transported to La Salina.

She stayed in a small trailer out in front of the Cantina over the weekend and then had to be driven back home on Monday morning.

Conchita was a wonderful cook and a great addition to the Cantina. She made absolutely the best Chile Rellanos in the world. Everything she cooked was great but there was one BIG problem. She was what some called "a one pan cook." That is she would only cook one meal at a time! A party of more than one person soon learned that the food would leave the kitchen one plate at a time. This process was slow, slow, slow and if you were hungry when you ordered you would be starving after watching everyone else in your party being served ONE PLATE AT A TIME!

If you complained Conchita would throw the pots and pans around the kitchen and start screaming at the top of her lungs. When she got into one of her moods the male waiters refused to enter the kitchen with an order. Hell not even the manager would set foot into that kitchen until she settled down. Jack tried once and she beaned him with a coffee cup. This was somewhat entertaining but it slowed the process even more. Jack bought her a full set of professional pots and pans and had a large commercial stove installed in the hope that she would use them and learn how to prepare several meals at a time. Conchita elevated her chin and absolutely refused to even consider their use.

No one was ever really sold on the fact that Jack really wanted to speed up the food service. If there were four people in a party it meant that you would all have at least two drinks before the forth person was served. Everyone learned to eat the food as it was served or the food would be stone cold before the last meal arrived. Proper manners went out the window when you were eating in the Cantina. Have you ever tried to eat Mexican food after the grease has congealed—Ugg!!

Jack finally solved this problem by hiring an assistant cook to help Conchita.

Why did the customers and management put up with this service? Simple! It was the only game in town. There was no Baja Mar Golf Course nor was there a trailer park. The only other place to eat was La Fonda's and that was a long and dangerous drive after a few drinks.

Conchita knew her value; she got paid good money, was transported to and from Tijuana, AND was given a nice trailer to stay in while in La Salina. No one else wanted to work so far from civilization.

The food was great; you just had to know before hand when you were going to be hungry so you could order your food in advance.

Conchita really didn't last very long. When the good cooks and waiters in Ensenada found out that the Cantina 'always' paid in U.S. dollars they were more than willing to drive the 40+ mile round trip to work here. Why? Easy! Every time the peso was devalued they in effect got a pay raise because their *gringo* dollars bought more and more pesos.

To this day the Cantina remains one of the only bars that continues to pay in U.S. currency. That's why we get such great people to work here in La Salina.

Jack

It had been a long time since Jack Speer had been a young man when he stumbled into La Salina back in 1963. Jack had been involved in developing entire new cities in the Los Angeles area after World War II. He knew the value of land and he certainly knew that La Salina would be a wonderful development in the future. He was on his last down hill run when he founded La Salina. This was his last hurrah.

The only structure in the place was an old adobe home that overlooked the white beach and the blue Pacific. After Jack made his 'deal' for the land, from the ocean to the 'old' dirt road to Ensenada, with the Arrellanes Family the modern history of the camp was launched. The old adobe evolved into Rancho Bensons Bar and then into a place we all know as the "Cantina."

When I began to catalog what others and I knew of Jack, I was surprised to find that none of us really 'knew' him. A lot of us knew a lot of things about him but none of us knew the <u>man</u>.

We would all watch in amazement, as Jack would make his entrance into his domain, the Cantina. He would shuffle in 'ala' Jackie Gleason, his arms flapping like a duck, his head and neck making like a "Do-Do" bird. He would suddenly stop, smile, and then go wide-eyed, letting the rest of his face go completely blank. He would swivel his head around, like a nervous crane, and peer around the Bar. Leaning forward at the waist, he would comb his hair back with his hand, laugh, turn and walk away—that was his entrance routine and it would never change unless he came in sober. It seldom ever changed.

The Mexican flower ladies loved Jack—he always bought 'all' of their roses and gave them to the women in the bar. One day Roma, his wonderful wife, was heard to comment that he never brought flowers for her. He had to be a real hard man with whom to live.

The Mexicans all loved Jack and he was always showing that he cared for them in return. If a family needed money for medicine or someone was getting married or someone died Jack was always there to help. He treated David Medina, the President of the Corporation and Manager of the Cantina, like a son. This was to cause numerous problems after Jacks death.

He owned a Restaurant and Bar in Downey California and that was the best place to find him if you decided you wanted to buy a lot. Only Jack would name a restaurant the 'Slaughter House.'

Once while visiting with Lu Ann he started talking about the Real Estate Brokers test he took shortly after graduating from college. Lu Ann, who is an R.E. Broker herself, was amazed when Jack confided that he had never studied for the test until he started cramming three (3) days before the exam and that he continued to pop 'uppers' or speed to see him through. He said he collapsed after the test, which he passed, and had to be taken via ambulance to a local hospital. He was chuckling like mad as he told this crazy story on himself.

Some of you may have heard that Jack never served in World War II. That was because he was one of the original $1.00 a year whiz kids who kept our war effort on track. You had to be a very, very smart cookie to perform in that rarified environment.

In the beginning I'm sure that Jack enjoyed his 'scotch', but by the time most of us became exposed to him his enjoyment had moved onto a basic need. It got to the point that he began to "talk in tongues." This really scared many of the women in camp. Fortunately, there was only one guy who could understand him when he began to talk in "code" and that was Russ Hopkins. Both Jack and Russ were card-carrying members of the Mensa Society and that I'm told certified both of them as genuine geniuses.

It was nutty! It didn't matter how drunk Jack got, the next morning he could recite chapter and verse what had been discussed the previous night. He might not know what had happened but he always knew who said what.

Russ was an amazing guy in his own right. He was 6'7" and weighed about 265 lbs. He had been a tackle for the Champion UCLA football team in 19__ something. He blew out a knee and that closed out a pro career and relegated him to the role of a bartender for the rest of his life. When in the clutches of demon rum Russ could and would recite Shakespeare from beginning to end with only a pause every now and again for little liquid refreshment.

Joe Patterson, of the Los Angeles Sheriff's Department, tells the story of he, his 'mother', Roma and Jack drinking on the patio in front of the Cantina when Jack complimented his mother on the beautiful, pleated, blouse she was wearing. She returned the compliment and admired the Hawaiian shirt Jack had on. As the afternoon wore on and they became a little more intoxicated, Jack offered to trade his shirt for Joe's mothers blouse. Joe said he was amazed when his mother and Jack took their respective tops off and traded right in front of God and everybody. Jack acted extremely pleased with the trade and pranced around the patio showing off his blouse. When Joe and his mother got ready to leave she asked Jack for her blouse back, he refused saying, "A deal is a deal." She went home with the Hawaiian shirt.

Few of you knew that after a night of working the people in the Cantina that Jack stumbled down Avenida Lorenzo and fell into a septic tank hole. He became impaled upon the 'rebar' that reached skyward from the unfinished hole. The steel punctured one lung and other less meaningful places on his body. It was after sunrise the next morning before anyone heard him moaning at the bottom of the pit. Jack's health moved down hill after this incident. During his waning days he took on more and more of the actions of the legendary Howard Hughes—it was uncanny! He stopped visiting with friends, and was constantly holding a tissue to his nose. He even started letting his finger and toenails grow long and curving. He became an almost total recluse toward the end of his life. After Jack's death his ashes were scattered in the ocean directly front of the Cantina. Over 200 of his Mexican friends attended the services.

A short time later his dog, "Lucky," died and was buried overlooking the spot where Jack's ashes were scattered. Wander out in front of the Cantina and you will see the head stone for "Lucky." Jack is just out there in the Pacific.

Were it not for Jack we would not be enjoying this "Little Bit of Paradise."

Thank you, Jack!

The Shootout at the Duck Pond

Not very many people remember that the Lagoon at La Salina used to be a stopover on the flyway from Canada south for many varieties of duck. They would stop here and replenish themselves after the long trip from Canada. In his book, "Arriba Baja", Larry Stanton, describes the lagoon at La Salina as a "nice little pot hole." This irritated me for a long time until I understood that he was not talking about the condition of the road. I guess he meant that it was a good little place to hunt the ducks!

The duck's arrival was a great occasion for the hunters and the wannabes who had places in La Salina and Angel's Camp. A few guys were extremely serious and even built duck blinds, but most of the guys were just having fun. It usually turned out to be a *muy peligroso* (very dangerous) place to be when several men from Angel's Camp would converge on the south rim of the lagoon while their counterparts from La Salina would take their places on the north side. Both groups were well armed, their shotguns loaded with birdshot. Most of them also brought along a bottle of their favorite spirits to fortify themselves for the rigor's of the hunt. Wild Turkey seemed to be the favorite with good old Jose Q a close second. This was definitely not a beer event! The fearless hunters rarely hit any of the ducks because by the time the birds arrived most of the guys were already seeing double and had a great deal of difficulty tracking the ducks. As a result

of their positioning around the pond it usually turned out to be a reenactment of the war between the North and the South. It was a common occurrence for guys on both sides to take direct hits from stray duck loads. The shot would not kill but they sure could hurt. One year three men, -two from Angeles and one from La Salina, had to seek medical aide in Ensenada. Naturally, the hospital reported their injuries to the local police. When they did nothing but laugh and tell the guys to be careful, both sides decided to return to the duck hunt the next morning.

Little did they know that the cops had asked the Mexican Marines to put a stop to this annual mayhem. The next day the hunters surrounded the lagoon to continue the hunt (war) only to find themselves surrounded by the Mexican Marines.

They began disarming (remember it is against the law for us to have guns in Mexico) the valiant hunters. After losing his shotgun, one wise guy told his buddy not to worry he had more guns at his house. Unfortunately, the officer in charge of the Marines overheard this comment and in perfect English ordered the wise guy to accompany him to his home where they confiscated three handguns.

No one was arrested but this action put an end to the Annual La Salina Duck Hunt. No, none of the weapons were returned to their owners—they just disappeared!

Uno Mucho Loco Gringo

Jim was a very pleasant guy who got along with almost everybody in camp nearly all of the time unless he had been drinking. Unfortunately, he was known to drink most of the time. He loved his rum and would drink it in any and all of its forms, straight, rum and coke with a twist of lime, in iced tea, etc. Hot or cold, it didn't matter he was always happy to drink it. This was not to say that he would not drink any other form of alcoholic beverage. I never knew him to discriminate against any liquid refreshment as long as it had a good dose of booze in it.

He even liked to mix something light in his coffee to start the day on a positive and pleasant note. Jim didn't mind drinking alone until mid afternoon. In fact, he rather seemed to enjoy sitting on his front patio with toddy in his hand and a good book in his lap as he watched the waves flow in and out. Around 3 o'clock you would see him out on the main street looking up and down the dusty road for someone to share a few drinks and some idle conservation with. The first person to come along would never be able to get past Jim. "Come on in and have a drink, sit and talk for a while. The sun will be going down soon and we can watch for the *"green flash."* It never appeared to bother him that the sun would not be going down for another 3 or 4 hours. He just wanted someone to share a few drinks and help relieve a little of the boredom in his life.

If he really liked you he would invite you to come back after dark to participate in one of his favorite pastimes—hunting in his vegetable garden. He would arm each hunter with a flashlight and an old kitchen knife and then the fun would begin. Jim would laugh, a real crazy chortle deep down in his chest, and inform all participants that the person who killed the largest, the smallest and the most tomato worms would each receive a prize! Try to visualize grown people, both men and women crawling around in the dark trying to find "Tomato Worms." Remember that in those days there were no streetlights to light the way. All they had was starlight and occasionally the moon would really make the hunt easy.

As I said, Jim was a very likable guy until he reached a certain point in his continual consumption of hard liquor. When he reached that point he no longer was able to act in a reasonable manner. His behavior became truly "*mucho loco.*" Some said that this was caused by the steel plate in his head, which he received as a result of his involvement in the Invasion of Europe in WWII. I'm not sure of that but let me give you a vivid example of his behavior and you be the judge. One night, in the early 1970's, Jim was drinking in the Cantina when two plain clothes State Police Officers began questioning a fairly young, good looking blonde. They searched her purse, found a baggie of marijuana and placed her under arrest. Seeing this, Jim slid out of the Cantina, ran to his house, got his rifle and hurriedly returned to the Cantina. He burst in and demanded that the *Polica* release the girl immediately. When they ignored him he pulled out the rifle and shot one of the cops in the leg. The place became a zoo—people stumbling over each other in an attempt to get out of his way. When no more shots were heard several people came to the aide of the wounded cop. During the confusion Jim beat it home, got his wife and rapidly headed north to the border. Jim never set foot in Mexico after this episode.

Oh! Yes, the State Cop that he shot in the leg is that wonderful, easygoing guy you all know as "Ramon Puente," my good friend, and the best bartender the Cantina has ever had.

Salud!

Liz Looks Around

Liz Beatty took a very circuitous route in finding the place of her dreams on the beach in La Salina. In 1967 she read, "How to Retire in Mexico on $2.75 a day." The author, Earl Stanley Gardner, said that the best place to retire in all of Mexico was in *Playa La Mision* in Baja California. With that in mind she and her seventeen-year-old daughter Kate, jumped in her car and headed for Baja. She looked in La Mision—no luck—and headed down the old road to Ensenada. They looked at several places, but nothing tickled their fancy. On their way back they discovered *Playa La Salina*. Liz said that a sea of bright yellow flowers underscored the whiteness of the beach and the blue-green of the ocean. This was it! This was what she had been looking for.

A few months later she got her husband, Doc, to drive down to La Salina. They ended up buying (30 year lease) an ocean front lot for $3000.00. That was in 1968. 1969 saw them start construction on their dream home. It was built for the princely sum of $4000.00.

The Beatty's early on became very closely involved with most of the Mexican families in the area and maintained that relationship for over three decades. Liz always made it a point to visit with each of her Mexican friends every time she returned to La Salina. She did not hesitate to take young Mexican girls, whom she had seen grow up, aside, and tell them—"to be careful and you are too young to get married." She cared about her 'friends' and it showed. When interacting with the Mexicans, her face would soften and take on a special glow.

Doc Beatty (MD) played a mean piano and he and Joe Connolly, playing the guitar, entertained the patrons of the Cantina whenever they were in camp.

Some of the stories Liz told were difficult to believe, not that they didn't happen, but that they happened to her. One of these was the time she was in a restroom of a bar in Ensenada when a Lesbian propositioned her. We'll not cover any more episodes here. Suffice to say, Liz lead not the sheltered life a lot of people thought she did.

When I began writing articles for the camp paper, the *"Que Pasa"* (What's Happening), it was Liz who suggested the by line of 'The Dirt Road Philosopher.' Most people would say that we were both wrapped up in our Liberal vs. Conservative beliefs—but they would be so terribly wrong. We loved to explore each other's beliefs (that's a neat way of saying arguing).

I sorely miss our quiet conservation's while she threw balls to her dog Judy on that dusty dirt road.

86

Whenever Liz was in camp on a Friday night, she made a point of going to the Cantina and having dinner and a few drinks with her old friends. She always ordered a Mexican combination plate because that 'was' the thing to do. She went to visit with her old friends but as the night progressed you would find her visiting with a 'new friend or two.'

Listen to Liz describe her "little bit of paradise" that she loved so much. "The wide, white beach ran for three miles with tide pools at each end, like book ends. The pools at Angel's point were like aquariums. In camp we found ground squirrels, meadowlarks, bunnies, lizards, and a few snakes. In the lagoon were Stilts, Mallards, Blue Heron, Phalaropes, and around the house were Humming birds, House Finches, Swallows, Ravens, Starlings, and a Marsh Hawk who patrolled the swale in front of our casita. On the beach were Least Sandpipers, Willets, Gadwits, Pelicans, and Gulls. The ocean contained hundreds of Dolphins with whales coming and going from Alaska to Scammons Lagoon."

Did she love this place? You bet! She hated it when the streetlights came in! She complained that she could no longer see her stars or the phosphorescent Naito-flagella (her words-not mine) that made lightening like streaks across the tops of the breakers in the moonlight.

Jack died in 1983 and the family moved back to their home in Berkeley, California. After her husband's death Liz would load up her car and she and Judy would make the trek from Northern California to La Salina four times each year.

While in camp, she always wore a perky yellow and blue bandana covering her hair. We would see her each evening just before sunset, sitting on her front porch-drink in hand-waiting to see "the green flash" that she and Doc had seen so many years ago; on their first night in La Salina. When she saw us she always smiled, lifted her drink, and silently laughed.

Just before her death in June of 1998 she wrote, "Memories of My Casita" which she ended with the following; "Jack is gone and my kids are far away, but I still have to come down to my casita because it is so beautiful, and it's mine."

Liz first came to La Salina during Easter week of 1968. She came back in 1998 to her final resting place; the ocean in front of 'her casita'.

We think of her often and always when someone mentions the "green flash."

Goodbye, Friend!

The Fisherman and His Bride

Jim and Lois Christie came to La Salina in mid 1969 and proved to be very popular and welcome additions to camp life. Jim had grown up working for the Southern Pacific Railroad. He started working as a day laborer when he was just 12 years old. He worked his way up through the ranks until he reached his lifelong dream when he became an Engineer.

Jim was a large, raw boned, Irishman who would laugh at the drop of a hat. He would also argue any side of an argument before the hat hit the ground. He would lean into his opponents face, with fisted hands on hips, and very gruffly and loudly advise him that, "you don't have the slightest idea about what you are talking." His stature, demeanor, and that simple statement won Jim most of his arguments without any further discussion. With the argument won Jim would put his big paw on his foe's shoulder and with that deep, gravely, voice of his exclaim, " come on friend I'll buy you a drink."

He was without a doubt one of the strongest men I had ever met. One time Frenchy, Harold, Jim, and I were trying to move a big slate pool table in Frenchy's house.

Two of us were on each end but we were having absolutely no luck in moving that monster. Jim called a halt and told the three of us to get on one end and he would handle the other. Well, Jim lifted his end and we all struggled with ours. That was when I decided that Jim could 'win' all of the arguments in the future.

He was really the best fisherman in camp and he kept in practice by driving his old, green, Baja Bug down to the beach where he would put in about four hours of fishing each and every day. He always came back with a mess of fish. We used to joke about the fact that the only thing holding that rusty old bug together was all of the fish scales, which covered it inside and out. You could smell his car as he went by. You could also hear him when he returned if you listened closely for the clanking of the empty Tequila bottles as he bounced down the road.

Like I said, Jim was a great fisherman and we could count on him and Lois putting on at least two and sometimes three fish fry's a year with everyone in camp invited. We would set up tables on the main road in front of their house and eat, drink, and enjoy each other's company for hours. In those, early, days there never seemed to be any hurry and laughter always seemed to bind us together as a group.

Lois, more properly "Mother Lois" was without a doubt the best cook this camp has ever seen. If you got an invitation to dinner at the Christie's you knew you were in for a treat. She was as slight and frail as Jim was large. All of the Mexican kids in area called her "nana" and she was the guest of honor at all of their birthday parties.

90

Lois had a way of making everyone she came in contact with feel comfortable and important. If you caught her and Jim at the Cantina she would always pat the seat next to her and with a great, wide, smile say, "come on over and sit with me."

As she approached her 82nd birthday her doctor suggested that she quit sipping Tequila. She was 86 years young when she passed away in the home she love so much. I closed her eyes as the Mexican men, women, children paid their last respects!

Back from Nam

Don was definitely not a handsome man. His head was way too large for his body, which was substantial. His ears were too large for his head; his nose was bent and did not fit his face. His face was always sunburned and it never to turned to a tan. His eyes were normally bloodshot, and he always had an astonished, wide-eyed look about him.

No one knows exactly how or when he arrived in camp. He was just 'suddenly' here. We do know that he left the Marine Corps as a Gunny Sergeant in late 1968 after two tours of duty in Vietnam and a total of 12 year's service in the Corps. Don spent the first couple of weeks sleeping on the beach with his dogs, one black and one red, nasty Chow dogs. No one could go near either of them. They slept with Don and guarded his camp while he was drinking at the Cantina.

Apparently, as with a lot of guys who returned from the jungle, he had a whole lot to try and forget. His answer to this was to drink, drink, and drink some more. After a couple of weeks his drinking slowed down a bit and he became almost human.

The next thing we knew he had built himself a "Hooch" on the property that is now considered to be Father Porro's. What is a Hooch you ask; 'well it is a cross between a slit trench and a 'home away from home'. It is what our guys in Nam lived in while at the 'front.' For a further, more in depth, description just ask any guy who served there. Don's hooch was about five foot deep and large enough for four or five grown people. It had a roof about two feet above ground level and a shelf dug into the side for his sleeping bag. By the time he moved into his 'home' he had three more dogs, a German Shepherd, and two just plain ol' mean camp dogs. All five dogs slept, with Don in the hooch and guarded it with bared fangs. No one, in his right mind, went anywhere near it.

As Don settled into camp life it was interesting to see the effect he had on many of women in the Cantina and around camp. Like I said he was NOT good looking but many women found him irresistible. He was a *'mucho macho con tipo'* and they loved him. Ok, it means he was a very manly, but a crazy, guy. Soon he and Shirley got hitched and fought each other for the next several months until they split up and went their separate ways.

Don was the guy who supervised the construction of the house for Chuck Schwartz who later sold it to Frenchy Theberge. Don caused the house to be partially built on McLaren's property. Not really a great problem, only the kitchen fell outside of the property line. None of us could understand how he got away with building houses in Mexico. He was obviously a gringo and he had none of the required papers to even remain in Mexico much less act as a contractor. He built that house and another one for Father Porro who lived in it until his death several years later.

Don eventually moved back across the border and no one, not even his ex-wife, knew what happened to him. One guy claimed he re-enlisted in the Corp and returned for another tour in Vietnam. In spite of his relatively short stay in La Salina Don is still remembered by most of the people who knew him then. He marched to a totally different drummer; a guy who made life move just a little quicker whenever he was around.

Shirley, his ex-wife, commuted back and forth between Los Angeles and La Salina in her small motor home. She christened it the "La Salina Shuttle" and everyone knew when she hit camp. You would always see it parked in front of the Cantina for several hours after her arrival. Like they say, 'it was a dry and dusty trip'.

Digger Dean

Dean Fluss was drafted into Army early on in the Second World War. He spent the entire war filling body bags in one campaign after another. This experience had a tremendously negative effect on such a young man. He came home a nice, but a little strange, young-old man. He drank a lot and then every once in a while he drank not at all.

Dean was a professional undertaker who gave many of the older Hollywood Stars their last makeup session. He worked for years at Forest Lawn Cemetery before he went into semi-retirement. Even after he moved to La Salina he was called back occasionally to make someone more presentable.

Digger always bragged that he returned to the States in First Class accommodations. It seems that they used "The Queen Mary" to transport our guys back from Europe after the war. First Class—I don't think so—they crammed over three thousand men into a space meant for about 1200 people. The trip from France to San Francisco took a very slow 28 days.

Dean and his wife came to camp in the late 70's. They bought an ocean front lot and built one of the larger homes in camp. A short while later they bought the lot next door and built a small casita, which they attached to the big house. We were all a little surprised when his wife suddenly left camp and moved back to Southern California. 'Digger,' sold the big house and moved into the Casita where he remained until shortly before his death.

Dean began (continued) to spend most of his time chasing the local ladies in and out of the bars in Ensenada. His first lady friend was a younger, very attractive native of Baja. She had a terribly explosive temper! On more than one occasion, while dancing and drinking with 'Digger' in the Cantina; she would walk up to some big gringo guy and knock him on his ass. She really enjoyed kicking the hell out of some unsuspecting guy. Rosa was one tough gal! We later found that she had been a professional woman wrestler in Mexico. Some said that she was part 'Yaki' Indian, all said to stay away from her when she got mad!

Once after a big fight with Digger she turned him into the *Federales*. When they came to his casita and searched it, they found his .25 cal automatic right where she said it would be. They took the pistol and they took him. We didn't see Dean for more than a few days.

95

It cost him a couple hundred bucks to get out of the Ensenada Jail. He never saw that gun again. He did see the lady wrestler a few more times before moving onto a little tamer woman.

Digger was a mild mannered guy who had an awful time with his alcoholic consumption. He just could not live without a woman at his side. He died a few years back and the camp has never been quite so boisterous since his passing. We think of him often.

Across the Pond

Peter and Mim, they were our English couple. They settled fairly early on in the history of our camp. At one time we had an English couple, a pair of Canadians, and two Australians. In addition to that we had a doctor, a policeman, a baker; but no; we never did have, a candlestick maker. We did have a lawyer, a priest, and another cop. We could birth you, marry you, divorce you, and if you were bad, arrest you. Oh! Yes, we could bury you too for we also had a mortician in camp. Well, I got a little off track on that, but to me it fit!

Peter had a shock of pure white hair and very bright blue eyes. He was always going a hundred miles an hour and never really getting anywhere. He had been a Royal Air Force flyer and flew in defense of England during the "Battle of Britain." That, alone, made him a very special guy in my books. Mim, his wife, was short, at the most 4'11", and weighed a good deal more than she did when she worked in the Burlesque Shows during the "The War to End All Wars." As was to be expected, Mim was a wonderful dancer, she always wore colorful Moo Moo's, and after she had a few she would really start to move. It didn't pay to get in her way when they started to play "The Stripper." Peter was not much of a dancer but when Mim started to go crazy with the music he just got a happy, slack jawed, look on his face. Guess he realized that one thing would lead to another. Oh! Yeah, she  was a wonderful cook who made the greatest 'kidney' pie around. The people in camp enjoyed her pie almost as much a Peter enjoyed her strip tease.

They owned the lot, on the ocean, at the north end of camp. Yes, after Heine and Dottie and before Jo and Alan Hicks. Unfortunately, Peter developed a very rare disease and they decided to move back to good Old England so that the socialized medicine system would pay for the expensive treatment. After waiting for two years for their number to come up in the lottery the English called medical care they moved back to Long Beach. They were great people and we were sorry to see them leave our camp!

Walt and Evanne were our Australian couple even though Evanne was born in Missouri. As with all Australians Walt was a hundred times larger than life and would laugh and greet everyone he met with a cheerful, 'ga day mate!' Following War II he returned to Australia and became a bush pilot. Later he took up professional motorcycle racing and made a good deal of money.

Walt was having a 'look see' around the United States when he met Evanne, they got married and he became an American citizen. He had been trained as a machinist so he opened his own shop to support his new wife. He became so successful that at one point he was making parts for the Apollo Space program and other programs that followed. Evanne seemed to be a typical happy go lucky blonde. It didn't take long to realize that while she could almost be as crazy as Walt—she was the real brains behind their success in life.

They never really settled down in camp but they did build a house and would drop in out of the blue every now and then. Suddenly they would stroll into the Cantina all dressed up like a couple of Texas Cow folk. Decked out from the white Stetsons on their heads to double stitched black pants tucked into their Tony Lama boots. When they walked into a room the energy level was multiplied ten fold. Walt loved to drink and visit with all of his friends until the bar closed. Whoever was left would continue to party at his house until early morning.

Walt would be up, after a couple of hours sleep, full of energy and ready to cook a complete 'Australian' breakfast. It was always great; his specialty was deep fried mashed potatoes. They were fantastic. Like nothing you have ever eaten.

Remember I told you that Walt had been a motorcycle and a racecar driver; well you took your life in your hands if you got in a vehicle with him. He never just drove—he raced—with one arm thrown over the back of the seat. He never seemed to watch the road as he was forever looking at and talking to the folks sitting in the back. You had to have several drinks under your belt before you felt even a little comfortable with him driving. Very few people ever 'raced' with him more than once.

Bill and Early Merrilees were our third overseas couple. Bill was a Canadian ands a partner of Walt's in his machine shop. Evanne told me that Bill had gone to the same café for 12 years and that he always ordered the same roast beef sandwich each and every day for lunch. Apparently not a guy to try anything new. And yet, he married a bilingual lady from the Philippines and moved to Baja for most of the later part of their lives.

Bill had been a Canadian Marine in WWII and had apparently been parachuted into France to assassinate a few people who were working for the German's. He was a very quiet man whose idea of a conversation was "Yep" and "OK." One day I noticed him sitting in his garage stropping a large knife. Looking closer I noticed that it was not just a knife—it was a dirk. When I asked him about it he suddenly reverted from character and told me the story of his exploits during the war. He showed me the calf-sheath where he had carried the dirk since 1942 when he  graduated from Canadian commando school. He told me that he had sharpened and oiled it every day since the war. You should know that a dirk has only one function and that is to kill people! He was a really great, quiet, guy, who knew what the world was all about.

Early was a wonderful lady who spoke English and Spanish better than most. Her ability in Spanish made her our unofficial interpreter in matters small and large. You needed to get the gardener to do something special, see Early. If you needed someone to read a legal document find Early. Always smiling and happy to help. A really strong couple and a positive addition to camp life.

If there were a problem with rowdy visitors in camp—look around—Bill would be standing behind you ready and 'able' to help.

A real comfort!!

Murder on the Beach

The Gringo's, a husband and wife, had left their kids with a sitter and escaped the rat race for a carefree weekend in Baja. They pulled into La Salina at about dusk. They had never visited the Cantina before but after a few drinks they were up and dancing like they had spent their whole lives in Baja. One thing led to another and soon they retreated to their camper that was parked on the beach in front of the Cantina.

Soon all of their 'relaxin' found them both stripped down and ready for action! Soon a loud banging noise interrupted them. Being totally involved with each other they ignored the noise. The banging got louder. Finally, the husband got up and opened the door and found two armed banditos standing outside. The big one started yelling at him in Spanish. The older, short guy told him in very broken English, "get out here and give us all of your money." The husband sort of staggered out onto the sand. It was obvious that he had no money on his person. Soon, his wife tumbled out of the camper naked as the day she was born. The big guy tried to grab her, his thoughts apparently had moved from robbery to other more basic things. Suddenly the husband grabbed the rifle away from the older guy. Swinging the gun with all of his might he struck the big guy on the head. This caused the gun to fire, wounding the husband and killing the older guy. The wife, still naked, ran, screaming, up to the Cantina.

After much discussion Señor Benson decided that his son "Petie" should drive the Gringo's to the first aid station at The Half Way House. He admonished his son to go no further than the aid station. This was because by Mexican law, the couple was involved in a major crime.

So, with "Petie" driving, the husband lying, bleeding, on the back seat, and the wife (still naked) in the passenger seat, they headed north. First they passed The Half Way House "and the aid station", then Rosarito Beach, then La Gloria's, and soon they hit the border. An alert Custom Agent noticed the wife and astutely judged that something was amiss. After brief questioning of the husband and wife he called an ambulance and sent them on to an American Hospital. The agent then notified the Mexican Police and turned "Petie" and the car over to the Mexican Officials.

The Mexican Police sent detectives to La Salina where they found the dead bandit still lying in the sand. The other guy was being held at the Cantina. Upon the completion of their investigation they threw "Petie" in jail for aiding and abetting two felons in leaving the Country. They also impounded the vehicle.

Several days later Señor Benson visited his son in prison and asked him why he had failed to stop at the aid station. Petie, looking rather sheepish, smiled and said, "I just kept looking over at that, beautiful, naked lady! She just looked so good—and you know I didn't want to stop. So I just kept driving and looking until it was too late.

This event caused an international incident and the Gringo couple never returned to Baja. The husband did send some money down to get "Petie" out of jail.

Oh, Yes! "Petie's" cousin was really pissed when they impounded his car. No, it was never returned. After that, "Petie" used to laugh and say, "it don't pay to try to help no naked gringo's."

The Streets of La Salina

The naming of the streets in La Salina is of importance for only one reason; they identify the real founders (*the pioneros*) of this "Little Bit of Paradise." They are a reminder to all of us who came later of those who truly enjoyed this camp to its fullest. They knew how to wring the most out of life and they sure knew exactly how to taste this wonderful spot along the Pacific Ocean.

Avenida Lorenzo was named after Larry Pearson, the husband of Peggy. They came to Mexico shortly after he suffered a major heart attack. He was told that he only had a few months to live. He stayed several productive years and Peggy stayed almost 30 years. Oh! Yes, he was the first to die so he got the big street named after him. Usually this honor would go to *Presidente Juarez* here in Mexico.

Next is Calle (Caye) Heine. "Heine" was a great fun loving guy who would take hours just walking to the Cantina from his trailer, which sat at the north end of camp. He built the very first water storage tower and shower in camp. It still stands and should qualify as a historical monument. At the time there were only 5 or 6 dwellings in camp and he would visit each and everyone to have a drink with his friends and to shoot the bull.

Calle Arturo. Named after the guy you all see in the large picture hanging in the Cantina. He's on the motorcycle wearing the serape jacket. Quite a man! His was the first house (the A-Frame) built and it cost, basically, nothing. That's another story that appears elsewhere. When the Toll Road opened most people-traveling south used the A-Frame as a landmark. Art's house was always a Party House and I'm very pleased to say that it still is and I hope it always will be just that.

Calle Jose. Which was named after Joseph Connolly. Joe was a retired concrete contractor from Los Angeles. He was, apparently, very wealthy and the story was that he had gold bars hidden in his garage in camp. He built the house the Duran's now occupy. The patrons of

Bensons all called him 'Jose' because he was always singing Mexican songs as he played his guitar. He was the only entertainment in camp for a long time. Don't bother looking for his gold. People have been looking, on and off, for many years with no results.

Calle Placier. This street was named after one of the Original Mexican members of the Corporation, Bobby! He was a very colorful individual who was always the life of the party in the Cantina and any other place he happened to be. He was also the Marshal of Ensenada for several years.

Calle Lolita. The only woman honored with a street. Lolita Kelly apparently landed in the "back bay" of La Salina sometime about 1946. She and Bertha Kline (both Americans) built the original house in La Salina del Mar—it became Bensons Bar and then just the "Cantina." Lolita's home is the giant white house at the east end of the lagoon. I am told that these two women were the first real party people in the area.

Calle Speer. This is the only street that the Community Group had a say in naming, and it was the last to be named. Jack Speer was the guy who came to La Salina in 1962 and had the good sense to realize it's potential. He started the Corporation and entered into a fifty-year joint venture with the Arrellanes Family in 1963.

Jack was the stuff of which legends are made.

Calle Berlo. Curly was a real power guy who built the big white house at the south end of camp. If you met him you would swear that you had just run into a real Don of the Mafia. He had pictures hanging all over the place of guys like President Reagan attending a 'bash' in his, Curly's, home in Hollywood. He is the only street person who is still alive. I hear he is now somewhere in Oregon.

All of these individuals were amazing people who would go out of their way to welcome you into 'their camp.' They would always show you how to really enjoy this "little bit of paradise."

Caballos (Horses)

The Game of Horses is the greatest leveler of people I have ever experienced. Gringo's and Mexicans played, guys could play and the women loved it. The rich could play and the poor certainly did. My grandkids love the game. They are only allowed to play at home. It is an illegal game in Mexico because it is a wagering game. The Federales were the only ones who did NOT seem to enjoy it. Caballos was the social event of the weekend at almost any family style Cantina. It was just plain, clean living fun; usually it accompanied by much laughter, some screaming and hollering, and quite a bit of backslapping. It also involved a bit of direct confrontation whenever a couple of players would get a little overly excited. No one ever got killed but occasionally it lead to some heavy pushing and shoving. Oh! Yes, for sure it involved a continual, moderate level of drinking or the bartender would politely ask a non-drinking player to leave the bar. The house couldn't make any money; they didn't get a cut of the play, unless the guys and gals paid for their seats by drinking some kind of alcoholic drink. Early on it was just beer or vodka and later it became beer and Bloody Marys.

This wonderful game required no special physical size or ability. It didn't even demand a large amount of intelligence. It surely did help if a person could count the spots or markers on five dice. AND it was a requirement that each player had a sufficient number of coins or bills in his pocket with which to wager. As the evening wore on most players would help each other call the result of their cast as the light got dimmer and dimmer.

If you have never played this game of chance then you really have missed a very basic ability to mix with the peoples of at least two countries. Namely, Mexico where the game is played and the United States that always seemed to provide a good number of players on any given weekend.

It is a very difficult to explain how it is/was played. The nuances of the game are such that no one could possibly explain all of its facets. You had to wager and play to gain any real degree of knowledge into how it is played and most importantly how the wagers are made. It is kinda like poker, but totally different.

Some people shake the dice in the cup like mad, then slam it down on the bar as they holler for—whatever. Others talk to the cup and then gently let the dice dribble out of the cup and onto the bar. You can still see indentations on the bar caused by the 'slammers'—no, not the drink!

As I said before it is played with five (5) dice which are marked with nine dots (nines) on a side, ten dots (tens), face of a court jester (jacks), the face of a queen (queens), face of a king (kings) and the shape of a spade or a single dot which represented an ace. Nines are the lowest in value and aces are the highest, you have to throw at least a pair to wager. Straights and flushes do NOT count. To play each player has to ante (usually a quarter or a couple of pesos) then, in progression, each player is allowed up to three casts of the dice, usually from a special dice cup, upon the bar in front of the player. If the player got, say, three aces in one cast-he would announce *tripe aces en un* (3 aces in one roll). With that he passes the dice, in the cup, to the next player to his right. By only casting once this restricted all of the following players to one cast or toss. A player has the option to stop at one; two or three tosses provided he had at least a pair. If a die comes out stacked one upon another then you had to roll again—that is usually when you had rolled three or even four of a kind. It really killed you to have to throw them away. The poorest possible toss would be a pair of nine's *en la noche* (all night or three rolls). The greatest hand is *cinco aces en un* (five aces in one). A wonderful hand would *cuarto reinas en la toto dia* or four queens all day (in three). Winning a few quarters doesn't seem like much but when you have 18-20 people each ante a quarter you ended up with a pretty good pot AND as the night progresses the quarters usually changed to paper stuff. Another aspect of the game is the side bets between individual players—say Lu Ann rolled three jacks in one then other players could challenge her by placing a "side bet" and stating *no mas jackes en dos* (no more jacks in two rolls). If she rolls another jack on her second roll she claimed all of the money placed on "the side bet." She was very good at that and it was not unusual for her to proclaim, after rolling three of a kind on one toss, *dos mas jackes en la noche* (two more jacks all night or in three rolls) thus placing a side bet of her own. Any other player could cover this bet. Needless to say these side bets could amount too much more than the original ante. Charlie Carbahal was a master at winning side bets even though he rarely won the main bet. He would make side bets on four queens (which he got so often you would have sworn that he was married to the ladies) get beat by *cuarto Reyes* (four kings) and still win on his side bets.

Tequila Pancho had a very unusual manner of playing Caballos! He would play his hand, then get involved in a side bet, usually with a new gringo, and start yelling at the top of his voice, *"yu cheet yu malo gringo I kil yu right now"* The new guy would normally back away and Pancho would giggle loudly as he raked in the money. He tried this with me a few times and when he found that I would not back down he would laugh, slap me on the back, and call me a *"cabron"* (a bastard).

I never understood why the game died out in the Cantina. Some said that it was the Federales but I never saw them close down a game in over 20 years of playing. Others said it was an American bar owner. No matter what the reason! When this simple little game died out so did a lot of the interaction between the Mexicans and the Americans and we all lost as a result.

Horses anyone?

Dirty Miguel

I have known Dirty Miguel for over 30 years and I have never known him to participate in what is commonly understood to be the activity of work. Once I did see him lean on the handle of a shovel for an extended period of time. One of the working guys whispered something in his ear and he suddenly dropped that shovel like it had turned into a hot poker. A few weeks later I asked him about this incident of almost work and he replied, *"Trabajo es no bueno por el alma"* (work is no good for the soul) "Oh, Señor Burnie, I almost committed a terrible sin— everybody knows that to work is not good for the soul." That was Miguel; he would do just about anything to avoid the stain of 'honest' labor.

Miguel did have a 'regular' job—really more like a position—as a gatekeeper at Campo *Mariposa* (butterfly).

110

He was a true *filosofo* (philosopher) who had gone beyond the needs of modern man. Or! Perhaps he had never acquired those needs that seem to afflict other, more common, people. He had no need to bathe and rarely did so. Changing clothes was a far to involved endeavor to occupy his time. He has been known to wear the same clothes for over a year. He might take his overskirt off if he got too warm. You immediately noticed the increased aroma and the fact that his undershirt was no longer white, it had turned to a mottled earth color as a result of continual wear. His boots once black were scuffed beige with use. His beat up old, plastic, kinda gray, cowboy hat never left his head unless it fell off or he went to bed.

Removing his hat was his idea of getting undressed. He got his hair cut almost every year and he shaved but rarely.

Miguel thought of himself as a regular *"Don Juan."* He was always asking the women in the Cantina to dance. This normally happened just after he became so drunk that he could hardly stand much less dance. He considered himself to be bi-lingual because he could say, "wanna buy me a drink." He proved his bi-lingual ability quite often. Miguel would remove his hat with a flourish as he asked the ladies, "Lady wanna dance." You could not help but notice the hay sticking out of his hair as he removed his hat.

Dirty Miguel was really a great guy and you could learn a lot from him—if the wind was just right—and you could get close enough to hear him. On a weekend you could usually find him sleeping in the weeds just down the hill from the Cantina. He usually started waking up when he could no longer avoid the glare of the sun shining in his face. Picture the sun and you will realize that this was just about noon!

Gus loved to tell the story of Miguel and one of his drinking buddies, he only had one at any given time, they just were unable to keep pace with him when it came to the bottle. It seems that Miguel and his most recent friend had

been drinking Tequila most of the night and found themselves lying in tall weeds at daybreak. A rattlesnake was making its way across Miguel's chest. Noticing the snake, his friend grabbed a half full bottle of Tequila and started to club the snake to death. Miguel suddenly awoke, seized the bottle, and screamed, "Don't do that! You'll break the bottle." At this they both started laughing, rolling around, and fighting for the bottle. The snake wandered off after biting Miguel. Seeing this, his buddy, of the moment; exclaimed, "We gotta get you to a doctor." Taking a great slug of booze Miguel just laughed! They finished the bottle and passed out again. No, he didn't go to the doctors and he never seemed any worse off for the rattlesnake poison. Apparently, one poison cancelled out the other.

Lots and *Lotes*

Sue Connolly, the wife of that guy, Joe, who supposedly had hidden gold bars in his garage, owned several vacant lots scattered around camp. When she, suddenly, saw a 'newcomer' beginning to build on one of "her" *lotes* she went ballistic. She challenged the poor guy and threatened to have him arrested for squatting on her lot. He produced a bar napkin that conveyed title to the lot; signed by Jack Speer—this was not at all uncommon during the early days of camp life. Jack would scribble the lot number, the date, down payment, and the total cost of the lot. This would suffice until his secretary could type up a formal lease agreement. Sure, it was kinda of loose but it normally worked. OK! Well, this time it didn't and Sue ranted at anyone she could find about how that 'rotten bastard' Jack had deliberately sold "her" lot and pocketed the profit. David Medina, then President of the Corporation, could not placate her because he found that Sue did own the lot in question and that Jack had sold it to a third party. David promptly put a stop to any further construction on the twice-sold lot.

You should all know that when Jack usually wandered into Camp he was normally well along the path to oblivion via demon rum. Jack returned to camp a couple of weeks later; and fortunately he was relatively sober. He readily admitted his error! He got together with the third party guy and got him to agree to move to another vacant, and unsold, lot by agreeing to reimburse him for the cost of the construction on the lot that really did not belong to him. Jack then contacted Sue and assured her that, "No harm had been done," and in fact the incomplete construction on her lot had actually enhanced her property with 'no cost' to her. Sue didn't buy that at all. Thinking that she had Jack over a barrel she had him hauled into court in Tijuana. Several of us ended up testifying that we 'knew' that this was just a simple paperwork mistake and that it was not a common form of doing business. After many questions the Judge threw the case out and advised Jack to pay more attention to business when he was selling lots. He also advised him to drink a 'little' less when conducting proper business.

This reminds me of the time Frenchy blew his stack when he found that the kitchen of his house was not on his lot and in fact was five feet over onto Art Mc Laren's lot. It seems that when Don Paschal originally built the house he had misread the northern property line. This was not very hard to do because in the beginning there were 'no clearly defined' lot lines. That's true! The ocean front lots were all supposed to be 40 feet wide by 100 feet deep (except for McLaren's which you'll remember was to biggest lot because he and Jack cast stones to determine its layout) but in reality some became 41 feet wide by 100 feet deep. Others became 38 or 39 feet wide. A few buildings are even intruding into the main road.

It really didn't matter (still doesn't) to most people, after all this is Baja. Frenchy never had gone along to get along. So he threatened to haul Jack and the Corporation into court.

A few days later Jack and Art were having a few drinks in the Cantina when Jack told Mac of his problem with Frenchy. Art laughed and told Jack that, "it was no problemo, just give the Frenchman six feet of my property and that way he can't complain and he can still wash his windows without coming onto my property."

So that's just what they did and another land dispute was nipped in the bud.

Building A Dream Home

So! You have let it be known, in camp, that you are about to start construction on you dream home. What an exciting time! Before you select your contractor you will save yourself unnecessary grief if you do two things. First have all of your plans drawn up by a licensed Mexican Architect. Occasionally they will use your plans but all of the language must be changed into Spanish and all of the measurements converted to meters. The Architect should also get your permits. Make sure that your contractor is paying Social Security for himself and his workers. If this is not paid in advance the penalty can be over 100%. Yes, you get stuck with this unnecessary expense. All of your neighbors in camp have their favorite contractor and most of them will visit you to extol the work of "their" *maestro* (master) builder. You talk to a few of them and decide that Chicho will be your guy. He will be the one to work the magic to make your *Casita* (little house) exactly as you wish it to be. Very quickly you will find that building a house in Baja is unlike building anything anywhere in the world. True! The basic skill and tools are the same but the approach taken by your contractor is original and unique to Mexico. He will usually only quote a price for a small

116

portion of the job at a time. A good deal of this is because the cost of materials swings rapidly as the peso is devalued. Let's say that he has given you an estimate for the sub footing, the main footing and the walls of your *Casita*. You have agreed upon his price and yet, he stands there with his arms folded across his chest. He will look at the ground, push his hat back upon his head, and shift from foot to foot. He is waiting for you to give him some of the money so he may start the job. You should know that in Mexico a handshake or a verbal agreement still means a lot—"like it used to in the States." Many contractors and even business people will become very offended if you ask for a receipt. Still, it is best if you keep a log of expenses. At the same time they do not like to discuss money. It is just not the thing to do in the Mexican culture. This is not a problem in a large city or a metropolitan area. But, you would not be building your dream home in one of those areas. Heavens no! You want to be right up front with an uncluttered view of the waves as they frolic upon the white sandy beach. Can't you just hear it now! The sound of the surf is so soothing to your soul as it blocks civilizations constant attempt to intrude upon your solitude.

Ok! It is up to you to figure out how much money Chicho will need to start the job and keep his guys working until you get back down with some more money and to see what progress has been made. This is a very difficult part of contracting. You have to control the money so that he does not get too much money ahead of you. If he does then he and his men are likely to wander off and have a fiesta. Then nothing gets done on your house. Or! If you give him too little he will work until the money for the materials is gone and then he will send his men home because he does not have any money to pay them. In either case you will be less than ecstatic when you return and find little or no progress has been made. If you have given him the proper amount of money you may still pull into camp on a Friday afternoon and find that Chicho and his crew are working on a job at the other end of camp. When he notices you are in camp he will come by and assure you that all of his guys will be working on your *Casa Grande* (great house) first thing Saturday morning. They will be! You will hear their music, hammering, and laughter by 7 o'clock. They will make a great show of working very hard until noon or even one o'clock.

Yes! The average Mexican workingman still works 44 hours a week. You will soon learn that without your more or less continual presence little real progress will be made on your dreams.

The Mexican appreciation of time is far different than is ours. It is not that they are they are lazy or indifferent. It is just that they know that your house will get done *sometime.* In the meantime other more pressing matters need their attention. Particularly, if you are absent and another client is standing there with money in his or her hand. They will work on that place until he or she leaves and then they might return to your job. This behavior boils down to the fact that they "honestly" want to make all of us happy!

By now you are finding that no matter how large, small, or humble the house in Baja it *is always a dream home.* You will find that it is not so much a house as it is a

Condition. It becomes a new philosophical approach to life itself. It involves a new sense of freedom, an ability to relax and let down barriers and to interact with and enjoy people. You will always describe your dream as *mi casita* (my little house) even thought you always think of it as *mi casa grande.*

Finally, you have reached the stage that the work on the footings and the walls are almost complete. You have even gotten over the shock that your house sits a little crooked on your lot and a couple of feet away from where you had planned for it to be. You are beginning to blend into Baja and realize that it is just *no big deal!* At this point Chicho politely informs you, he prefers to do this through a third party, an interpreter (somehow this seems to make the meeting less direct and somehow more pleasant). He tells you that due to things beyond his control it will cost you just a little more than he thought to complete the next portion of the construction.

You don't really have any choice at this point unless you want to walk away and give up your dream. Even if you were willing to walk you would have to contend with your ego, your family's desires, and a whole lot of other things. How do you go back to the States and tell your friends that you have been a fool and that you didn't realize what you were getting into by trying to build a house in a country where you really didn't appreciate the rules, customs, or language.

Chicho makes it easy on you because he has a finely developed sense of how far he can go in this little game. He will only increase the cost a *little bit* and the price will

119

still be within the ballpark of what you 'knew' it should cost.

Now the walls are up and you have learned a great deal, that is if you are smart and do not have more money than good sense. You know that you have to 'drop' in on your construction unannounced and a various times during the week. Never tell your crew that you <u>won't be down for two or three weeks</u>. This just gives them an okay to work on another project until you return. You realize that it would be even better if you hauled a trailer down and stay on site for a few days or a week at a time. This will allow you to be fairly sure that the work will go ahead on schedule.

Something to remember that will make your contractor think you really are starting to learn about the rules in Baja—never give him or any other Mexican a check. When they take an American check to the bank in Baja they will have to pay 10% of the amount of the check to cash it AND they may have to wait up to two weeks to get the money! Always pay in cash AND in U.S. currency. No pesos! They will love you for understanding this. So will your neighbor because some old timer will end up cashing your check for their *amigo* and then they will have to wait for the transfer to take place even in the States.

Now that you are forced to spend a little extra time in Paradise you will be able to get some fishing in with your kids. Or surfing, or just wandering on the beach and talking. You may even wander up to the hub of the camp-the Cantina-have a few beers and meet some new friends. Should you bring your spouse, or whomever, you can make a point of going out to dinner and dancing the night away. Who knows, your marriage, or friendship, may grow just as your dream house does.

Wow! This is getting easier with each passing month (only kidding), the roof is almost finished and Chicho is after you to decide what kind of tile you want on the floors and countertops. You favor the rustic, genuine, Mexican tile and he tries to talk you into going with a good Italian tile. You may like the rustic stuff, but he is right. A few years of wear and you will find that it acts like a blotter. It will absorb anything and you will wish that you had listened to him. Now you have to start thinking about the bathtub, toilets, sinks, stoves, etc. Let Chicho do the tile work for a good size tub and shower. You buy the glass doors and fixtures in the States. They will be cheaper and of better quality. Same with the toilets, sinks, faucets, and all of the appliances.

You are now set to embark on one of the National pastimes of Mexico, *smuggling*. The Federales may not think it is funny but it really gets the old adrenaline fired up. You buy the stuff and try to hide it, then you time your trip across the border to increase you chances of sailing though the border without stopping to pay duty. That is a real dirty word to the guys who have been around for any length of time. One guy spent 20 years smuggling big stuff into camp for anyone and everyone. At last count he had smuggled fourteen TV sets, seven stoves, three freestanding fireplaces, nine refrigerators, and a bunch of other stuff. He just got a kick out of outsmarting the Federales!

Don't be alarmed if you turn your cold water on and find that "C" is really for *Caliente* (hot). Some of the guys still hook the water lines up in a manner in which we believe to be incorrect. Don't argue, just wait and reverse the lines later. Should you decide to install security bars think about placing them inside the windows, particularly, if your house is anywhere near the ocean. They are guaranteed to rust if they are on the outside and they will have to be painted at least three times a year for "ever."

Well! You have come a long way, your dream is not finished but at least you can move in and relax for a few days.

It's funny but houses in Mexico are never finished. There is always something to do, but don't let that get in your way of enjoying the sun, fun, and the people.

Welcome to Baja and please do yourself a favor, continue to learn about this wonderful culture. After all that is why you decided to build your *Casa Grande*.

Disfrutar! (Enjoy!)

Peddlers in the Camp

The Lobster Man was the first and by far the most important peddler to hit camp. He drove an old Chevy pickup. It was a basic green in color; one fender was white, another was yellow and the left rear always looked like it was going to fall off at the next bump. Ben, that 'was' his name, would wander into camp on Friday night just before dusk. He would stop in front of the house and holler, "You wana buy bugs—buy bugs." He'd reach behind the seat and pull out an old brown burlap bag crawling with fresh, live *langosta*. Louder he would ask, "You wana buy bugs! A dozen por benty dolars. No? Ok, Ok, $10.00 señor. Oh! Señor, No, No, oh No! OK, *Diaz* (10) *por* $5.00. NO! Only dolars, US, no *pesos*, only *dolars* señor." All this while his head and eyes swiveled in every direction. His eyes never left the dirt road into the camp.

I never understand his furtive behavior until I learned that the Mexican Government had created a monopoly when they formed the Marine Co-Op to 'buy all' of the local fisherman's catch for resale. A few of these guys, like Ben, realized that they could make a whole lot more money selling their lobsters and sometimes abalone directly to the visiting gringo's. Never mind that he could end up in jail for selling 'illegal', not short, langosta. Believe it! Fresh, live, lobster for 50 cents apiece. That is a small part of why we started calling this place *a little bit of paradise.*

The original Tamale Lady also wandered into camp early on Fridays. She was a little old Mexican-American lady and she always carried two pots of tamales covered with green and white-checkered cloths to keep them warm. Sometimes they were beef or potatoes and carrots. Occasionally they would be *pollo* or *papas* and raisins. Always they were four for a dollar—no pesos. More importantly! They were always delicious!

Once in a while she would show up with her pots of tamales on a Saturday and rarely she would show up on Sunday morning. I couldn't understand her erratic Saturday and Sunday visits. I finally asked her why. She told me that she lived in Campo Lopez, K-58, and that she and several other American ladies always played poker on Friday and Saturday nights. She said she loved to gamble and that she only sold tamales so she could afford to play. If she lost money on Friday she would get up early Saturday and make a batch of tamales so that she could gamble that night. If she won, we lost—no tamales and she slept in on Saturday. If she lost all weekend she would make some on Sunday morning to see her through the next week. She was no spring chicken, she had lost most of her teeth, but she still had a twinkle in her eyes. She was one of those numerous gringo women who had, for many different reasons, settled in Baja.

We realized that "the tamale lady" was no more when she missed several weekends. They said that she had won a big pot just before she passed away. She was 84 years young. Her name was Celica Lowbaugh.

Madera, Madera was the cry and you would hear it early every Saturday morning. If you had forgotten what day it was—not unusual in Baja—you knew it was Saturday when you heard the call, Firewood, Firewood. Usually it would be one of the Crostwaites in his well-maintained truck loaded with oak that he had collected on the ranches in the hills behind La Mision. How much you would ask and he would always reply, "Sixty *dolars es por todo.*" He always settled for $40.00 because that is what he wanted to begin with. You always had to beware because it looked like a good deal until they started unloading and you found two tires and a couple of empty boxes under the wood. This has happened time after time but the same guy has been selling firewood in this camp for over 20 years and No! You don't get to keep the tires or boxes.

The produce lady arrived on Thursday a little after noon. She drives up the coast from south of Ensenada selling her home grown, organic, vegetables in one camp after another. The ladies in camp insist, that no matter what she has, it is far better than what you can get in the stores. If you have looked at vegetables in the markets you know that they are absolutely right.

Yes! We now have a new tamale lady. She always comes on Sunday mornings and her tamales are great—same four for a dollar—but they are smaller. Her young daughter makes change while her mother smiles that Mexican smile. What is a Mexican smile? Well, let me tell you they are different, they start with the lips and spread to the eyes, they flow through the whole body, they flow directly from the heart. You are truly blessed if you have received such a smile.

The daughter who is no more than 5 or 6 years old is always very neatly dressed and she also possesses one of those smiles. I believe that she collects the money because her personality generates good tips. Once I overpaid her and when she gave the money to her mother she realized that I had given them to much money. They both came running back, laughing all the way, to return my overpayment!!

The regulars in camp don't really need a calendar. They can tell which days it is by who is selling what. As to what time it is that does NOT really matter. You can look at the sun and get close enough. If you are hungry you eat and if you want a drink you wander up to the Cantina.

The peddlers are an interesting bunch of people. Should you take the time to talk with them you can learn a lot. Not only about what they have to sell: but also about the Mexican way of life.

Mooning the Camp

At a point in time our beach was a Mecca for campers from all over California—and parts of Arizona. It was the place to be on any holiday weekend! It was not at all unusual for us to have as many as 200 campers directly in front of our normally peaceful homes! Three wheelers, quads, motorcycle, and dune buggy's roared from Clams Beach to Angels Camp non-stop. Oh! Yea! They did stop at the Cantina for a round of 'slammers' after every couple of circuits. Then they would all be off in a cloud of dust. This went on until 3 or 4 o'clock in the morning.

It was humorous to watch people wander over behind the dunes to relieve themselves. They would look up and down the beach to make sure that no one was looking, then they would squad and go. Unfortunately, the women would always leave those little white tissues to dot the beach until a strong wind could blow them away. After a while it got to be disgusting to be "MOONED" by people who apparently didn't even see all of the houses looking down on their bare butts. Once several campers parked directly in front of my house and the first thing they did was dig a hole in the sand, behind the dunes, and erect a two-sided privacy screen. Yes! You got it—the open side faced our home.

That evening Lu Ann and I had a few people over to watch the sunset and have a few drinks. This was a routine in camp. We all enjoyed looking for the 'green flash' as the sun sank into the Pacific. It was our one moment of serenity and peace in an otherwise 'hectic' day in camp. Soon our attention and conservation became focused on the two sided 'privacy screen.' We were all wondering how the people on the beach could possible miss the fact that all of us had balcony seats looking down upon their sand boxes.

Well! After a few drinks I decided to do something to let them know that they were littering our view of the sunset. I got out my rocket launcher; we all had them for

setting off fireworks. Carefully, I sighted it in on the privacy screen and fired off a Roman candle. A perfect shot—it landed just short of a guy who was squatting there.

Suddenly he <u>noticed</u> us! He yanked up his shorts and came running up the path; screaming at the top of his lungs. We were all laughing so hard we could hardly understand what he was saying. He had one arm in a cast and he was waving about it over his head while he held his pants up with his other hand. As he got to the top of the stairs, a very proper Peggy Reagle arose and greeted him with— "Well, just T-S, just T-S young man! You just may NOT continue to Shit in our front yards!" The guy looked around, then down at his half-mast pants. He turned and left without comment. You must know that no drunken young guy is a match for a not so prim and proper, retired, third grade teacher.

The Lady and The Gun

Barbara Dodd never really lived in La Salina. She did spend enough time in the Cantina to qualify as an honorary member of the camp. Barbara and her husband, who was a Lieutenant on the Los Angeles Sheriffs Department, built a beautiful home overlooking the cove at Angeles Camp. Sadly, they were only able to share the good life for about six months after he retired. He passed away very suddenly. She sold their dream home and left

129

the area. No one had the slightest idea what had happened to her.

Suddenly on one of those nights when it was dark, cold, and windy outside, she stepped back into the warmth of the Cantina. We all heard that laugh it was deep, sad, and mellow. We knew that Barbara had returned without even seeing her. That was how unusual her laugh sounded. After a few drinks shared with friends, who cared, her laugh became full bodied, throaty, and—happy! That was when that wonderful lady became "Barbara Tee Hee" to all her friends in La Salina. It was great to hear her laugh; everyone knew it and it made you—well happy!! She wandered in and out of camp life for years before she followed her husband.

The following brief story will give you an idea of how she met life. Always head on and always with a laugh

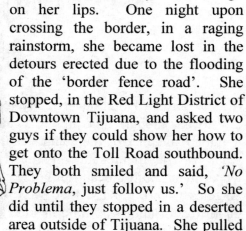 on her lips. One night upon crossing the border, in a raging rainstorm, she became lost in the detours erected due to the flooding of the 'border fence road'. She stopped, in the Red Light District of Downtown Tijuana, and asked two guys if they could show her how to get onto the Toll Road southbound. They both smiled and said, *'No Problema*, just follow us.' So she did until they stopped in a deserted area outside of Tijuana. She pulled in behind them. They got out of their car and approached

her car to tell her that she now belonged to them. She responded with a hearty laugh as she flashed her dead husbands' police badge.

When that didn't stop them she pulled his .38 caliber service revolver and cocked it. This they understood—no problemo—they were gone.

She found her way home and entered the Cantina soaking wet, but with her 'tee hee' lighting up the place.

It was crazy and no one understood how she got away with it; she carried her late husbands badge and gun in her purse—in Mexico; throughout the rest of her life. She not only enjoyed life, she laughed at it.

A Not-So-Nice Sam

Sam came to La Salina in the early 80's and purchased the oceanfront lot next to the 'A' Frame. He started building what we all came to call the 'Taco Bell' house. It looked like a drive-in and it was constructed of all red adobe blocks. Thus the name. Sam started bending the rules as soon as he bought his lot and never—ever stopped tromping on them. As we all got to know Sam we came to the conclusion that he rarely if ever thought that any rule could possible apply to him. He got around the one story height limit for the houses in the front row by building the first story underground. It was amazing to watch him operate.

The first thing we knew he had a very large bulldozer working on his lot. He had bribed the operator to dig his lot down ten feet and push all of the dirt out toward the Pacific Ocean. This expanded 'his' lot about 75 feet west of his property line. God! What guts. The equipment operator worked for the Federal Highway Agency and the giant bulldozer belonged to the Government. This was only the first of numerous actions on Sam's part that caused him and the 'Corporation' to butt heads. This continued, in a grand fashion over things both large and small, for several years. The people on either side of his lot were not at all happy over his actions. It left them with the land under their respective homes starting sluff away undercutting their houses. When they approached him about the problem he just laughed in their faces and told them it wasn't his problem. They were forced to build retaining walls to support their homes.

When he built his monstrous house he extended it exactly to the property line on the north AND then he built his pump room for his water 'on' the Widow Pearson's property—where it stayed until he died. No! He never asked permission and he had to trespass every time the pump needed repairs. Sorta tells you how Sam responded to those around him. He didn't! He just went ahead and did what he wanted.

One of Sam's first actions was to have a 'house warming' at his trailer. This even before construction was begun on his house. He impressed almost everyone when he pulled out elaborate plans for the construction of a resort in San Jose del Cabo. The plans showed that he and a past President of Mexico were partners in the endeavor. He talked as though they were *compradres* (best of friends).

Sam told everyone that if anyone in camp needed a favor he had the necessary pull to help. We soon learned that the only person he ever pulled for was Sam. I'll not name the *Presidente* because we were sure that he was not even aware that his name appeared on those fabulous plans. Yes! That is all they were ever to be—just plans.

Sam had been wandering around Baja for a few years before he landed in La Salina. He was always trying to impress everyone with his vast knowledge, which somehow never seemed to stand the test of time. The one thing most of us admired in him was the fact that he never stopped trying to come out on top on every 'deal' he tried to complete. He knew more *abogados* (lawyers) than a man should need and he always seemed to need them.

Whether he was just walking down the old dirt road or approaching you in the Cantina you 'always' felt that you should grab a hold of your wallet and hold on tightly!

He had an idea that he could build a 'city water system' by taping into the Arrenallos Well. The well was on the east side of the Toll Road. He wanted to install a large water tank that would gravity feed the water into camp. The next thing we knew he was operating a 'ditch witch' to dig trenches for water lines throughout the camp. You guessed it! No warning. Several of us were trapped.

133

We could not drive over the trench he had dug across the front of everyone's property.

The Mexican workingmen went bananas. "That machine wasn't legal in Mexico. Sam didn't have a permit to work in Mexico and they were going to try and get him deported. He was taking jobs away from the workingmen." He just grinned, that misshapen side of the mouth grin of his, laughed, and continued doing what he wanted to do. He even dug a trench across a Mexican Federal Highway and got away with it. Anyone else would have been in the

back seat of a black and white taxi being escorted across the border. A few of us said the system wouldn't work but Sam proved us wrong. It worked quite well for several years before it had to be upgraded.

The Mexican Authorities did send him across the border on at least two occasions and he was directed not to return to Mexico. It is really hard for a *Norte Americano* to get deported from Mexico but Sam managed it more than once and with little difficulty. Like a bad penny he just kept showing up back in camp.

After his wife died he began to drink even more heavily than normal—which was a lot. With his increased alcoholic intake he became an even nastier 'old' man. He was thrown in jail on more than one occasion.

One time he had driven to Rosarito in a very drunken condition. The police stopped him at the Toll Booth because he had been driving the wrong way for over twenty miles. After being questioned by a Mexican Highway Patrolman. Sam was about to get a free ride, because of his age, when he suddenly pulled out his—and pissed all over the officers shoes.

They not only tossed him in jail they also impounded his car. After he got out of jail it took him about a month and over $400.00 to get his car back!

Sam finally passed away in his mid 80's. I'm told he was still trying to work a deal. He was 'always' a very devious and optimistic fellow.

A Gentle Giant

Marco was a large, friendly man. Looking at him you could easily see that his Mexican heritage had been positively impacted by those Irish deserters who had jumped ship at the turn of the last century along the coast of Baja California. When he smiled, which was often, his gray-green eyes would light up and you could see into his very soul, soft, friendly, and caring. He carried himself with an easy, natural dignity.

He was a man who really liked everyone. His slow smile caused all of those around him to enjoy his passing.

He was a wonderful bricklayer, a true *maestro*, and if you were lucky enough to have him tile your roof you <u>never</u> had to worry about it leaking. A hard working man, his shirttail was always flapping in the breeze. He was constantly tucking his shirttail back into his pants.

I will never forget the time he was laying bricks at Sam Worthington's new home. Sam had been watching him and began counting the number of bricks Marco laid in a given day. When Sam asked him why he only laid 50 bricks a day Marco stopped, straightened up, pushed his shirttail back into his pants, looked at Sam, smiled and replied very quietly in his broken English.

"You only pay me to lay 50 bricks. Señor, I can lay many more bricks. But, then you will have to pay me <u>more</u> money sooner. In the end the house will cost the same."— Sam quit counting. Marco smiled and went back to work.

Over the years Marco developed a problem with booze and other more serious things. His shoulders began to slump and he moved with much less vigor. He still had the Irish smile and it still caused his face to glow. The smile came less often and when you looked into his eyes you still saw his soul but it had become enveloped in a soft hurt and a muted sadness that never went away.

After a few years Marco left the area and we lost a good and gentle friend!

Condenar!—Damn!

Visitors from the Sea—Shipwrecks

The old timer's in La Salina know that, on a foggy night, the cove at Angel's Camp looks enough like the entrance to Ensenada Bay to fool the skipper's of many a ship. The first shipwreck I saw was a beautiful, old, wooden, sailing schooner that had sailed into the clutches of those monster lava rocks just south of the beach. Its rigging had been torn away and lay dangling over the port side. The incoming tide caused it to continually smash against the side of the stricken boat. Finally, someone cut it loose and it floated away and onto the beach. The ship was never to move from those vicious rocks. The Lady was locked solid. This wreck occurred during a very foggy night in April of 1969. A work of art she, had been, until that terrible night. Her deck was of solid teakwood, the portholes solid brass, and her pilothouse sported gimbaled brass lanterns as running lights.

When the Insurance Company was notified they dispatched a Maritime Surveyor, from Long Beach California, to determine if she was worth salvaging. After a few hours of study he determined that it would not be possible to float her off those clutching rocks. She was written off as a total loss.

A few days later we watched, from the comfort of the Cantina, as many antlike creatures appeared and began creeping from rock to rock. Soon they were able to climb aboard that doomed old schooner. With the aide of binoculars saw that many Mexican men were using various pieces of old lumber to create a walkway from the shore to the side of the ship. By the end of the first day they had removed all of the fancy brass fixtures. Next the teakwood deck was torn up, piece-by-piece, and carted to the shore along with the wheelhouse. The next morning, at low tide, they returned to dismantle the ships' diesel engine and its drive shaft. All of this heavy equipment was manhandled over slippery, wave tossed, rocks and onto the beach. Trip after trip! The men worked like this for several days until only the ribs of the once beautiful schooner could be seen through the waves. They were forced to stop their salvage work with each incoming tide.

I've often wondered what happened to those gimbaled brass lanterns!

The next shipwreck occurred just south of *Salsipiduedes* (literally get out if you can). The cliffs here are some of the steepest, most dangerous, and rugged anywhere in Baja. A Mexican Naval Captain ran his Destroyer at full speed up onto the pebble-covered shore at the base of these giant vertical cliffs. He and several of his officers were last seen climbing those cliffs as they disappeared into the hills north of Ensenada. No wonder they were in such a hurry to get lost! That destroyer represented one seventh of the entire Mexican Navy! The ship rested at the base of the cliffs for several years. Finally, the waves battered it into nothing but a large rust stain. That was in the early 70's and you could see it easily from the toll road if you knew where to look.

The next visit was from a Japanese tramp steamer, the Uno Maru. It ran aground about a hundred yards south of the Cantina, about where the entrance to the Marina is now. This old rusty bucket was high and dry on the beach. It provided great theatre for those of us who watched the several rescue attempts. We had front row seats as we sipped our drinks in the warmth and comfort of the Cantina.

Day one found the Japanese Captain making his way to the Cantina in an attempt to determine where he and his ship were. He thought they were somewhere in Todas Santos (All Saints) Bay. When he found he was in a place called La Salina he cussed for a while in his broken English and then he decided, 'what the hell' and ordered a drink. He had a few more before he returned to his ship to radio his location to the Port Captain in Ensenada.

Day two opened with two small, ocean going, tugs approaching shore at high tide. They placed tow cables onto the grounded ship and labored mightily to free it from the sand. It was sitting in about two feet of water. They pulled and pulled to no avail.

We all laughed and chanted, "I think I can, I think I can." After working for several hours to free the ship a cable from one of the tubs suddenly snapped with a loud

140

twang and wrapped itself around the propeller of the other tug.

The powerless tug began drifting helplessly closer toward the beach. Was she going end up next to the grounded steamer? No! Quick action by the crew of the

first tug pulled her away. Giving up for the day they headed back to Ensenada.

Day three found the beach full of people just milling around the solidly stuck freighter. Some of them were shouting back and forth with members of the crew.

Day four opened with an extremely high tide anticipated for 1 o'clock. At 10 o'clock the two small tugs returned with a large, monster, ocean-going tug. They all worked to get lines to the stranded ship. When the incoming tide caused the old freighter to move they all began to pull. They would pull, then let the steamer wallow about, and then pull again. This went on for a couple of hours. At last! With a great sucking sound the streamer wallowed slowly out to sea. This was in the mid 1980's.

Several years later I was talking to one of my Mexican friends and I learned something about the Japanese ship which none of us were aware while she lie upon our beach. The Mexican guys had found that part of the cargo consisted of numerous cases of 'Sake.' They had traded lobsters, mussels, and clams for cases and cases of 'Sake' a Japanese rice wine.

Back in the late 1800's large wooden rafts were used to ferry produce, cows, etc. from Oregon and Washington to San Francisco and points south. These rafts were pulled by ocean going paddle wheelers. The rafts often broke loose and the remains of several of them have shown up on the beaches between Clams Beach, north of La Salina and Angel's Camp directly to the south. Most of the remains were just bits of wood and great steel spike like nails that were buried in the sand.

While dredging for the Marina they found a complete skeleton of one of those old breakaway rafts buried in the sand. They anticipate using it as a centerpiece for the Main Entrance to the Marina.

Several small powerboats have littered the beach over the past few years and most of us believe that these boats had been used to deliver drugs for trans-shipment north. The last of these to hit the beach came ashore directly in front of the Cantina. The story goes that the guy

142

who waded ashore from this wreck had been seen, further north, hauling bulky packages from his boat to the shore in a rubber dingy. A woman had been waiting for him with a four-wheel vehicle on the beach, just north of the Baja Ensenada RV Park. Anyway, his powerboat broke anchor and he lost his dinghy as he returned to his boat. The next thing we knew his boat was bouncing along southward in the surf. It left pieces of itself from the trailer park to the north jetty.

The guy scrambled through the surf and ran up to the Cantina. He was soaking wet and exhausted from his battle with the ocean. Ramon bought him a couple of drinks to warm him up. Suddenly, his teeth still chattering, he bolted from the Cantina and ran back down the beach and splashed out to his grounded boat. He spent several minutes looking for something. Shortly after he returned to Cantina he simply disappeared. The story became embellished to the point that it had him and his lady friend leaving the area with $27,000 in cash.

The boat had neither name nor any identifying numbers. The salvage of this boat was left to persons who will remain unnamed. The Cummings Diesel Engine now powers a Mexican big rig. The solid brass propeller has been turned into a wonderful coffee table.

Various other items are here and there. The remains of this large powerboat bounced around the beach for a few weeks before Mother Nature cleaned up the mess. This was in the late 1990's. I wonder how many ships will visit us in the 21st century.

Primo Tapia

Some people call it *Cantamar* (song of the sea); others apply the name Puerto Nuevo (New Port). To the Mexicans it is still *Primo Tapia* and that it always will be. I've asked several friends exactly what it means and no one seems to really know. If you look in the Spanish Dictionary it leads you to understand that it means prime or main wall but where does that leave you—still don't know! One old timer told me that it meant, 'low mud wall.' Oh! Well, who cares? I first got to know it as Puerto Nuevo back in the very early 60's when it was less than a dot on the map. The only thing to cause you to slow down as you rounded a wide sweeping curve at K-53 were word of mouth tales of wonderful *langosta* dinners that were cheap and served family style in the living rooms of the homes of local fishermen. The lobsters were always *grandes* (large) not the *chica* (small) ones they serve now. You got the lobster and all of the rice, beans, and tortillas you could eat for about $1.95 U.S. Beers were only 25 cents a bottle and sodas were a dime. To keep a running 'tab' of drinks served the empty bottles were left on the table and were only counted at the end of your meal. It was ok to wander into the back and get yourself another bottled drink, just don't take an empty with you. That was before Señor Ortega brought refrigeration to the small fishing campo. When you ordered *Langosta Puerto Nuevo Style* you knew that the lobster was fresh from the sea because they had no way of freezing them. Now you get 'Bugs' that are up to six months old, dried out and small enough to finish in two bites. The place is still world famous mainly because the new crowd of Europeans, Japanese, and young gringo's don't know what they are missing. <u>That's only half true</u>! It is still a fun place to take people who have never tasted the flavor of Baja. Most of the old houses are gone and the new restaurants are two or three story places where they charge you at least $16.00 per dinner and rush you out so that those waiting in line can spend their money. No longer do the fisherman's wife or her young children serve you. The kids are still around but now most of them are the wealthy owners of the new establishments. The soft and friendly family approach is no more. Oh! Yea. A cerveza is $3.00 U.S. and a coke is a buck and a half. Consider yourself lucky if you can find a place to park your vehicle.

The place I learned to call Cantamar is where I first began to buy adobe bricks for the patio in front of my trailer. It was and still is an individual family business where the bricks are handmade in the hills directly east of Puerto Nuevo. Very few of the families would or could deliver their product because most of them didn't even own a vehicle much less a truck. The bricks were only 2 cents apiece but you had to pick them up.

I made numerous trips into the hills to buy a few hundred adobes at a time. I almost croaked when someone in camp told me that they had gone up to 6 cents apiece. This drastic increase took less than a year. That's what an influx of crazy gringo's will do to prices. I bragged around camp that I knew "Old Juan" pretty well and that I was sure I could get the bricks for much less than the new price.

The next time I came back down I stopped in Rosarito Beach and bought a bag of Mexican soft candies and a quart of Tequila. By the time I left Rosarito it was getting dark. When I pulled up in front of "Old Juan's" small house it was very dark. In those days the only streetlights you would find in Alta Baja were in Tijuana, Mexicali or Ensenada. The headlights on my truck provided the only illumination.

I gave the candy to Juan's eight kids. He and I toasted each other with the Tequila and visited for a while. Soon we got down to business. Squatting in the dirt road in front of my truck he would write a price in the dirt and I would counter with my stick. At first he wanted 7 cents a brick; I was shocked! I countered with 2½ cents. We had another drink and he started lower and I went a little higher. Suddenly, I heard voices coming out of the surrounding blackness. I looked up and saw 8-10 young guys forming a ring around us. I became very uncomfortable when they started making very blunt and unfriendly comments.

Juan and I continued to scratch prices in the dirt until we agreed on $10.00 U.S. for 250 adobes-about 4 cents a brick. There were several stacks of bricks right next to my truck but Old Juan jumped in and told me to drive

146

further up into the hills. The unsmiling young men jumped in the back. This had never happened before and I became very uneasy. It was darker than dark, no moon and no stars, pitch black. We past many stacks of perfectly good adobe bricks as we drove further and further up into the hills. I became ever more nervous as we passed many Mexicans living in camps with brush and cardboard forming very rudimentary shelters. The only light was from campfires that were burning in each primitive campo.

These people had only recently come from the interior of Mexico in search of a better live. To these Indians Baja held out the same dreams as California did when people advised, "Go West Young Man!"

At last Old Juan had me pull over at the last stack, which lay hidden from the world at the dead end of a canyon. I didn't think that the night could get any darker. I was wrong. When we stopped in that small valley I could barely see the men as they jumped out of my truck. By that time I had hidden my wallet under the seat—stupid!

Had they wanted to they could also take my truck and if I were lucky they would let me to walk the eight miles back to La Salina. The guys started loading my truck and I stood by counting the adobe bricks. Now they were all laughing and joking and I decided that I would live to make another deal in the dirt.

With my confidence in the basic goodness of the Mexican people restored I laughingly pointed out that they had shorted me 10 bricks. Juan roared and told them to give me 20 more. I do believe they were just testing my ability to count!

I began to call it *Primo Tapia* when my good friend, David Medina, became the manager of one of the more successful maquiladoras in town.

The community had started out as a fishing campo with farming back up the valley. The two to three hundred souls had grown to a few thousand hard working people. It still hosts one of the oldest *Norte Americano* settlements in Baja.

Residents of Primo Tapia brag that they have the only fire department between Rosarito Beach and Ensenada. They also had the very first Police Station in the area.

So call it what you will. It is rapidly becoming one of the largest little towns in Alta Baja

The Old Time Cowboy

Cowboy Jim was a very unusual character in a camp of characters. He was slim, about 5'7", and walked as if he had a ramrod for a spine. He always wore a gray Stetson hat, faded Levi's, a soft blue shirt and an old Levi jacket. His brown boots were worn down at the heel and they always looked as if he had just stepped in a cow pie. No one knew where he lived or even if he had a place in the area. We didn't even know if his name was really Jim. He was a fair weather bird and we never saw him if the sun was hiding.

He would enter the Cantina at about 4 o'clock on a Friday or Saturday afternoon. He would walk to the bar, pull up a stool, and order a drink. He never said anything that you could hear. He just pointed at the bartender and set his open hand gently on the bar. The bartender always knew to pour him a whisky neat. This done he would take a long, slow, sip, push his hat back on his head and slowly survey everyone in the bar. Just like a scene from an old John Wayne movie. It was strange because he looked like a simple, old, balding Oklahoma dirt farmer. When he took in the ladies around the bar you immediately knew that his hat should have been a dark black.

He would just sit there and nurse his drink, saying nothing, until some young blonde honey would wander over and sit next to him. He would incline his head and touch his hat as she arrived. Cowboy Jim was no kid; his weathered face put him close to 60 years old. You had to watch very closely to see what would happen next. He would smile and pull a cloth bag—like an old Bull Durum Tobacco sack—out of his jacket. He would then flash his stash of marijuana for the young thing to see. He'd leer at the gal and they would be out of there.

He usually dropped the girls off sometime during the following day. This went on for about ten years and then Cowboy Jim disappeared and was seen no more.

Hunting the Octopus

One afternoon Cayo came by the house and asked if I would like to join him and his brother Joe in *"caza de pulpo."* I had not idea what in the world he was talking about. What the heck, he had asked me go with him several other times and I always learned something about Mexico and had a ball doing it.

"Sure why not!" I kinda thought that he was talking about fishing because he kept saying *del mar* (the sea).

The next morning he and Joe, a short Mexican version of "Hoss Cartwright," came by to pick me up. That is they came by, got into my pickup, and told me to drive over to the Mercado in La Mision Village. No, we were not going fishing because no one brought fishing poles. Joe crawled in the back; he was just too big to fit in the cab. I still didn't know what we were going to do. I became even more confused when Cayo told me to buy some "*blanquear*" and some cerveza. The beer I understood but what was "*blanquear.*" Turns out its bleach. So I got a gallon of that and a case of Modelo. When I got back in the truck I asked Cayo what in the Hell the bleach was for—he just laughed and Joe popped a *cerveza* for each of us.

We headed to the cove just south of Angel's camp. Parking on the cliff overlooking the rock-strewn beach we each had a couple more beers as we waited for the tide to go out. We wandered down to the rocky cove.

Cayo carried the beer, I had the bleach, and Joe had an old burlap bag draped over his shoulder. We talked for a while and I suddenly understood. We were hunting for octopus! But what about the bleach? Cayo took the bleach walked over to a half submerged rock and poured some of

the bleach next to it. Our first pulpo came roaring out. Joe grabbed it by an arm (tentacle), slammed it against a rock, and stuffed it into the bag. This went on until the bag was so full of octopus that only Joe (Hoss) could carry it back up to the truck. You guessed it, octopus hate bleach. Not a very fair way of hunting, but if you know any Mexican guys then you know that harvesting *comida* (dinner) is not a game!

With our caza over we relaxed on the rocks and talked for a while before heading back to camp. Cayo showed me how to clean the pulpo and I got to take a few of the tentacles home as my part of the hunt. I had a wonderful time! I learned three new words that I almost never have occasion to use and I made Octopus Stew for the potluck at the Cantina that night.

This trip reminded me of the time Lu and I stopped at Raul's Restaurant many years ago. It was during a time of tension at the border, the Mexicans were threatening to stop all Americans and make them get inoculations (I don't remember what for) before entering Mexico. You can guess that Lu and I were about the only gringo's wandering around Baja on that weekend. Anyway, when we stopped at Rauls Café and Yolanda asked us if we wanted to try some fried Octopus. I said sure and Lu just turned away. When I asked Yolanda how she got the octopus she said that she just dove down and stuck her hand in a hole in the underwater cliff and an octopus would grab onto her arm. I asked her what she would do if a really BIG octopus were to grab her arm. She looked at me as if I were an idiot and said; "you don't put your arm in no BIG hole."

Enough said!

Jose the Gardener

Up until 1984 all water consumed in the camp had to be hauled in by water truck. Cayo was the man for our camp and he made a very good living for his family by hauling water to various camps in the area. Soon a water system was developed that imported water from a well over near the mesa. This allowed water to be piped directly into our pillas. When this water became available most people in camp stopped buying water from Cayo. A few of the old timers refused to go on "the City Water" because we didn't want to hurt Cayo by reducing the money he made to support his family.

One day Jose stopped by my casita and asked why I continued to take water 'that way' pointing to the water truck. I explained that Cayo was *mi amigo*. I thought Jose would drop his question, but no, he continued to pursue my thinking in using that 'old way.'

"You know, how you say, progress it is a good thing. When I was a boy the tractors came, they could do the work of twenty—no a hundred men. You know people were afraid that they would lose work. But, you know, that didn't happen. They made more jobs. Yes! Progress is good." Leaning on his hoe he cocked his head and looked at me for a response.

"True," I said, "but you know Cayo is *mi amigo, mi comparde*. You know that I can't stop taking water from him because it would be like taking food out of his kids mouths."

"Ok! Sometimes progress comes too fast, but it is still good, *Muy Bueno*."

"Poco-poco" (slow-slow).

"Sure, OK! You know I went to the States in 1958. I worked for Pep Boys and made good money. You know I was in Tennessee and Alabama, all over. You know they didn't care if I was a Mexican, only if I was a good worker. I made good money. You know the United Way—I gave! I saw a lot of poor people in Tennessee. "I gave them money."

"Por Que? Why!"

"Because you know, they needed it."

"Oh!"

"I came back to my village in Mexico." They have a saying—*Elephantes* come home to die. They told me, "Jose you are an elephant!"

155

"Before I left you could go into the orange groves and pick oranges for *nada.*"

"In *los Estados Unidos?*"

"No, no in my village. But, you know, now the farmers have helicopters and voices out of the sky say 'Don't take my oranges'. Is that progress?"

I laughed and Jose said he had to go to work. He started to leave but turned and said, "It's crazy us Mexicans go to the States to work hard and make money. You gringo's come to Mexico to slow down and relax. But, you know, in the end all elephants return home."

"Si! I said, "It's a shame we can't take the Mexican heart and the gringo head and make people who truly think with both."

He looked at me, cocked his head and laughed.

"Si! That would be true progress. But, now I gotta go back to work!"

Ladies of La Salina

From the very first time I visited Baja I have had an image that seemed to just flirt at the edges of my conscious mind. As we drove down the old, "Free," road I would look over and see a carload of females heading south. I always wondered what drew them down here. Did they realize what they might be getting into by traveling south into the 'wilds' of Lower California? They started coming, even before the advent of the Toll Road and they have never stopped. They seem to follow that road as though drawn by a Mexican Pied Piper. No, they are not all young and they surely were not all what you would call "vamps." They were tall and short, slim and well rounded. Mostly they were a more seasoned bunch of people, but none of them acted as if they were anyone's grandmas. They were women and they seemed to know exactly what they were looking to find.

When I first came to La Salina I was ignorant of the fact that it was two women who had made this a 'party time' place way back in the late 40's. Bertha and Lolita were their names and they form the basis for the modern history of this bit of paradise. Almost 60 years ago they gazed out over the blue Pacific and knew exactly why they settled in La Salina.

Their sisters continue to flock to the shores of La Salina. Some come to bath in the sun, while others come to imbibe in the Cantina. Some do both! It's amazing how many of them returned to the States to gather their husbands or lovers and returned to Paradise where they staked out their claims to tranquility, sun and fun. Some came alone and remained that way! They knew better what they wanted than most. For the most part they were "professional" women. A large number like Peggy Reagle, M.C. Menzie, Jan Day, Eileen Swete, and Niva Gribble were schoolteachers. A couple were nurses. Some were involved in real estate. The rest represented a cross section of womanly pursuits from restaurant owner to hash slinger. Some were 'just' housewives but what women they were—they took a back seat to no one. Shirley named her Motor Home the "La Salina Shuttle." Thelma ran the bar!

I was a little surprised when I re-read "God and Mr. Gomez" and found that it was Mrs. Jack Smith (Denny) who insisted that they check out the land deal at La Bocana. She was the one who told Jack that they needed a sense of adventure in their lives. It was she who made the writing of one of the greatest books ever written about Baja possible. "God and Mr. Gomez" was the 'bible' for many of us who decided that we wanted to live with one foot in Mexico and the other in the United States. Most of our worries were reduced to laughter as we read that 'bible'!

It was Mr. Gomez who reduced all of our fears of owning (leasing) land to its simplest form—He told Jack Smith that the house would be his when he gave him the key. So simple! So clean and clear!

The ladies of Baja all had one characteristic that was the bedrock of their being—they knew what they wanted and they were unafraid of grabbing it!

Shortly after her husbands death Peggy Pearson and a friend, Patty, threw a few things in their bags and walked out to the Toll Road where they flagged down a 3rd class Mexican bus. They boarded and headed south to the *Bahia de Los Angeles* where they were to spend a few weeks on the beach fishing and visiting with friends.

Returning to camp Peggy said that it was a trip that she would never forget and one that she would never attempt again.

She spoke of kids with leaky diapers, chickens in the overhead and a live pig that kept farting. Patty said that the trip took just a little over 26 hours with the bus stopping constantly to pickup or drop off passengers. Peggy commented that, "I have never had so many butts pushed in my face." They were both thankful that the bottle of rum they carried aboard lasted 'almost' the whole trip.

The Sea Kayaker

I have come across many unusual sights while wandering up and down the beach at La Salina. I have found women sun bathing in the nude and men wandering around in the altogether. I have found glass floats, cork fishing floats of every style, size, and color. Driftwood by the cord has been lugged home. Broken diving masks and shattered surf boards were not that unusual. Other people's shoes by the gross (always the wrong size). I have even found unexploded naval ordinance.

Nothing, however, prepared me for what I stumbled across one day just after daybreak. Approaching the north end of the beach I saw a fairly large man who appeared to be attempting to set fire to his boat.

Getting closer I realized that the boat was a large ocean going kayak and the guy was just trying to stay out of the wind and light a single burner Bunsen stove in order to heat his morning tea. When I told him what I originally thought he was trying to do he laughed and admitted that on numerous occasions he had, in fact, thought about burning his boat.

Brad Meyer's was his name and he said that he had chucked everything a few months back and left his home in Anchorage Alaska to fulfill a lifelong dream of kayaking around Baja California. He smiled a lot as he told of taking five years traveling along the coast of Alaska in a 'small' kayak to prepare for his adventure around Baja. Brad was no kid; he had to be between 40 and 45 years old. He readily admitted that he might have read too much "Tom Sawyer" as a kid.

He shocked me when he admitted that he had no idea what the name of this area was. This surprised me and I became even more amazed when he told me that all he had to navigate with was a "Road Map" of Baja! Unbelievable!

I took him up to the Cantina and introduced him to Dick Harrison the manager. When I told Dick about "his map" he just chuckled and shook his head.

We had coffee and then Harrison shuffled back to his office. He returned and gave Brad a large book containing all of the latest nautical maps of both Baja and the Mexican mainland. Like I said before, Dick is one big cream puff.

Several months later a letter arrived at the Cantina from the Kayaker. Brad told of how he had completed his dream voyage, and that he had decided to try his luck in wandering south with the idea of going around Central and perhaps South America. He closed his letter by saying that he would stop by La Salina on his way back to Alaska.

It was crazy! Brad reminded me of may of us who think we can navigate our way through life with only the most rudimentary road map.

Stewards of the Cantina

This is just be a thumb nail sketch of the many people who have owned or managed The Cantina from its beginning in the 1960's up to the turn of the century.

Señor Benson and his son "Petie" you have already met. They are the "in the beginning guys."

Ramon Ballistros had been a rather famous Mexican boxer before he took over the Cantina for a short period of time.

162

Eddie Lopez was the young bartender that you also have met earlier on. He managed the place until he fell from favor and returned to Ensenada.

Thelma Flores came to La Salina in 1971 with Stan. They built the small house at the north end of Avenida Lorenzo. Stan was quite a musician and he was a wizard on the piano. He played in the Cantina for some time. Thelma is one of those people who always end up standing upright no matter what life throws at them. She spent many, many, years in Mexico-both on the Mainland and here in Baja. At one point, before she took over the Cantina, she had her pelvis crushed when some drunk driver pinned her against the wall in front of the Cantina. As the manager she came up with several changes that increased business—such as chili and hot dogs and Monday Nite Football. Even though she 'was' a Mexican citizen, she gave up her American citizenship when she married a Mexican man, the Macho guys in the Cantina did not like working for a woman. This was not true of "Ramon" the guy she hired and who is currently Jefe Ramon a wonderful man you should all know. She managed the place until she had a terrible argument with Jack Speer. Thelma moved back to the States when she turned 83.

Charlie and Mary Carbajal. This couple really enjoyed people and it showed. Charlie was a wonderful dancer and the women (all of them) loved to dance with him. Charlie had been a Tijuana police officer during the prohibition. Yes, he was that old! He used to smuggle booze from TJ to Hollywood in an old 1920's model Packard. It had a fifty-gallon tank hidden under the floor.

The stories he told would fill two books. Charlie was the guy who was responsible for introducing "The Bloody Mary Punch Card" to the Cantina. Each time you bought a Bloody Mary the bartender punched your card until the 50 numbers were obliterated. Then you turned the card in and received a 'free' T-shirt with wonderful artwork about La Salina. One of the shirts read; I DID IT 50 TIMES IN LA SALINA. This went on for several versions of T-shirts and many, many drinks. They finally stopped the program when they found that one of the guys in camp had purchased his own punch tool!

Mary, in her earlier years, was a model—did you ever see the slinky blonde in a black cocktail dress on the Billboards, all over the United States, advertising "Black Velvet Bourbon"—that was Mary. By the time they began running the place she had more than doubled her weight. Still, she was quite a woman and everyone enjoyed her company. She had a gravelly voice and when she laughed, which was often, it rumbled through the Cantina.

Next came another couple Dan and Sara Dean. Dan was a great big guy who was heavily involved in the day-to-day operations of the bar. Unfortunately, one day he literally threw a *cholo* (Mexican gang member from the States) through the front door of the Cantina because of his nasty attitude.

This bad little guy came back with a bunch of other little gang members and attacked Dan with knives. He was stabbed in the back and cut very badly. Phil Soto tried to come to Dan's assistance and Phil ended up in the Hospital in Chula Vista with multiple stab wounds and a punctured lung.

After the Dean's left Jack Speer took over the Cantina and named David Medina as the manager. David was also the President of the Corporation, *Constructores Pioneros de Mexico, S.A.,* in those days. After Jack died David was removed from the Cantina and the Presidency of the Corporation. David was and is my friend and most of the people in camp liked and respected him.

Jack Rotar became the manager under the new owner Larry Speer. Mr. Rotar tried to increase business by making it a "counter culture" type bar. Gone were the soft comfortable touches—replaced by filthy writing all over the walls. Most people in camp quit frequenting the place under Mr. Rotar.

Last but not least is Dick Harrison. Dick's motto seems to be—"I don't get involved, I just run a bar." Dick has cleaned up the place so that it is again a comfortable place to visit. He is the guy responsible for the kid's playground in front of the Cantina. Before he took over running the Cantina he owned the King Neptune Bar in Seal Beach. Dick is an old Mexican hand and he has owned a house in San Quintin for many years. He will probable not like my saying this, but he is really a great big pussycat who in his own ways has helped the community on numerous occasions.

AND then there were Smiley and Bang Away, a couple of real characters! I'm sure that I heard their real names' years ago but these were the two guys who furnished us with the music that we, in fact, danced the Night Away to for several years.

Smiley played the piano and Bang Away beat on the drums. They were there every Friday and Saturday night almost from the beginning.

The music they made together was really fun and most people could not resist jumping up to dance. They could play anything from Zorba the Greek to Rock and Roll, with a waltz, a polka, or Good Mexican Music thrown in. After they had a few it became very interesting –they would either start skipping a beat or change the beat or both all in the same number. They provided a lot of enjoyment for a whole bunch of people for a very long time. Those of us who knew them <u>and</u> their music miss them both.

Tequila Pancho

Pancho was not a large man but when he entered a room everyone noticed. He had a way of tilting his head, squinting his right eye, and giggling as his right hand lightly covered his mouth. His greeting was always conveyed with a crooked sort of a smile and a twinkle in his eyes. You had no doubt that this guy was genuinely pleased to see you. He usually acted as though someone had just whispered a slightly off color joke in his ear.

Tequila and his wife managed the first trailer park at the north end of the beach—Clams Beach. This area was in use by fishermen way back in the 1950's. Then you got there by traveling along a terribly rutted old dirt road that ran west to the beach on the south side of The La Mison River.

I first met Pancho in the early 70's. He knew everyone from Rosarito to Ensenada. If you wanted a load of good firewood go see Pancho. He could get you a pickup load of mahogany and oak turnings from a furniture factory for cheap! You needed a large propane tank, see Tequila Pancho, he could get you one for less than the Gas

Company could sell it. You wanted a pig for a barbecue see him. He could and would get you almost anything that you needed and normally for less than anyone else.

You obviously figured out by his name that he was a very hard drinking man. He was also a gamble-alcoholic who would bet on anything. 'I bet you' could have been his middle name. He loved to play *Caballos* and he would cover side bets of $5.00 up to $100.00. He laughed like crazy as he rolled the dice. If he won he would pat you on the back and holler, "*Si, Si*", and laugh. If he lost he would glower at you and call you a "sum bitch." Then he would throw his head back and cackle as if he had won.

Most people didn't know it but he <u>always</u> carried a pistol with him—most of the cops knew he had a gun but they never bothered him. On a couple of occasions I

accepted his invitation to play poker at his home. It was too much for me. The table stakes scared me a little but as the night wore on he re-earned his nickname. He became wildly funny until he pulled his gun and started shooting holes in the roof. This usually resulted in his wife charging out of her bedroom and screaming at the top of her lungs. More often than not this brought an abrupt halt to the card game.

Pancho lived his short life to the fullest. He filled it with many friends from both sides of the border.

Via Con Dios!

Bruce Willis in Baja

Halloween Eve! That was the night our dreams were tarnished forever. It would prove to be the last time that the doors to our Casita were to remain unlocked. I had gone for a walk through the camp at dusk as I always did, particularly, after being absent from camp for a while. But lets listen to my wife, Lu Ann, as she told her story to the State Police in Ensenada on the following morning.

"A guy in a ski mask came to the front door, he just walked in. We never locked our doors. I asked him if this was some kind of joke. I didn't even see the gun until he shoved it right in my face. He told me to shut up or he would kill me! He looked just like Bruce Willis, the actor. I asked him if he was the guy who stole our TV last week. He got really pissed and started waving his gun around. I shut up! He wanted to know where my purse was and I told him I left it in our truck because of the theft of the TV. I told him I didn't have the key to the truck and that my husband had it." The cops then asked her for a complete description of the bandito. "He looked just like the movie star Bruce Willis." None of us guys knew who Willis was at that time. She then told them, "he took my ring off and held it up to the light, like a jeweler would. I told him it was a fake. He just smiled and put it in his pocket.

He again asked when my husband would be home. I told him that I didn't know. He got very nervous and threatened to kill me. He kept telling me that he knew that I had more money than what he had found in my purse— He *knew* I had more! I argued that my husband carried all of our money. He got real mad and told me that he would kill me if I didn't give him the money—I got real scared when he forced me into the bedroom. You're not going to hurt me are you? I thought he was going to rape me! He said that if I didn't give him the money before my husband got back that he would blow my brains out! AND that he would kill Bernie too. I pulled out my purse, removed the $500.00 and gave it to him. He left and I just, sort of, melted into the couch."

When I returned from my walk I notice a car with no license plates, parked under a tree just south of our house. I didn't really pay a lot of attention until I entered our courtyard and noticed that the blinds on the kitchen window were pulled down. For some reason I didn't just walk in. I peered through the louvers and saw a hand holding a revolver and it was pointed directly at my wife. Being a working "Cop" I suddenly felt very naked because I had no weapon—remember it is against the law in Mexico (as many want it to be in the States) to carry a pistol. Suddenly, my blood began to boil! This guy had violated my house AND he was threatening my wife. I realized that I could not just barge in without putting my wife at further risk of injury.

I ran to my truck and got my combat knife. I was returning when he suddenly burst out onto the patio. He ran south through the yard next door. I was over the six-foot wall, on the north, in a second—now it would take me a week. I ran around our garage toward where I had seen the car earlier. As I rounded the corner the car burned rubber as it backed out in a cloud of dust. It struck me in the leg as it sped off. I noticed that there were "two" guys in the car. One of them I recognized as an American ex con who lived somewhere on the east side of the toll road.

The entire camp poured out into the street when they found out what had happened to LuAnn. They mobilized and made a complete search for the banditos. Even Cayo and Jack who had not talked to each other for years were in the same truck looking for the bad guys.

The next morning we gave the State Cops $20.00 for gas so that they could come out and investigate an "armed robbery." We waited for two days and they never showed. We both felt doubly used at that point.

I could never prove that the ex con had fingered Lu Ann but when two years later the Mexican cops caught "Bruce Willis," the ex-con returned to the States and has never again been seen in Baja.

We later found that the guy who robbed LuAnn had killed a man in Florida a few months before. Two weeks after robbing Lu Ann he killed an old guy in *La Playa La Mision*. That is only about 3 mile north on the beach from our camp.

Even with the ski mask LuAnn was sure that the robber was a gringo. She told him, "You're not a Mexican, a Mexican would never treat a women the way you have treated me."

This incident caused several changes in our lives—bars on all the windows and doors. Three security alarms! We now have a password that I use <u>every time</u> I leave the house. "You're locked babe."

It was a lousy Halloween!

Illegal Aliens in Mexico

I had been straddling the border between Mexico and the United States for over thirty-five years when I found myself confronting a true Catch-22 situation. For more years than I care to remember I have gone through the "dance" of getting and renewing my FM-3. I call it a dance because everyone who has gone through the process will either say it was a piece of cake (they are delusional) OR it was the most confusing and time consuming activity they were ever involved with. If you are fool enough to do it yourself you 'might' find that you can breeze through the process in four to six days. Much more normal time will involve twenty-one (21) plus days and numerous trips from your home in the States to the *Officina de Migration in Baja*. This is after you have visited the *Consulado de Mexico* that is closest to your home in the States. If this happens to be Los Angeles they will be much to busy helping their own people to worry about a gringo wishing to become legal in Mexico. San Diego is becoming even worse. Hope for San Francisco or anywhere away from the border or large populations of Native Mexicans within *Estados Unidos Americano*. Your first visit to the

Consulate in the States will require proof of income, certified by a Mexican Notario, and a letter from the Chief of Police/Sheriff stating that you have no criminal record. Then you will have to pay a fee to cover the paper work to this point. Next you will have to journey to the *Officina de Migracion* in the County in which you're (Mexican property) is situated.

Once there you will stand in line until at last you stand in front of a clerk who will require that you submit all of the papers that you paid for at the Consulate in the States. You must also provide a copy of your current lease and it must be in Spanish. She will then require that you fill out numerous other forms. Normally, they will just give you the form numbers; tell you how many of each is required (on this day). She will then direct you to a stationary store where you must purchase the 'government forms.' You must also provide passport photographs, black and white only—although once in a while they will accept color. When you have completed them you will, must, return them to the clerk. She will then check them for accuracy and return them to you so that you may take these forms to the Bank where they must be properly stamped after they allow you to pay the Government. Sometimes they will only accept pesos occasionally dollars might be ok. Once you get 'all' of the forms stamped—and you pay a fee—you return them to the clerk where you started. She will shuffle your precious, stamped, forms and then she will remember that you must take this 'new' form to a Notario for validating. This news may occur the same day or it may occur after you have traveled another 150-200 miles to pick up your completed FM-3. They honestly believe that retired gringo's have nothing better to do with their time. If you are lucky you get to wait around for the Notario, pay him and then return the stamped forms to the Immigration clerk. She will tell you that they must review your application to date! So you get to drive home and come back down in a couple of weeks!!!

It is a cat and mouse game and they love to make you dance! You can almost hear the music in the background as you leave the office.

Now you're asking why bother with all of this stuff. Well, if you have a lease on bare land in Mexico you may need to have an FM-3 to be legal (most of us gringo's don't think of ourselves as being illegal aliens) in Mexico. If you own a house for sure you are supposed to have one. Having an FM-3 gives you 'legal status' in Mexico. Without one you may be denied access to the Mexican Court System. Most landlords are not hot for you to possess one. If you don't have one then you are at their mercy! Reality is that a high percentage of Americans do not have the proper documents. Just as a high percentage of Undocumented Mexicans in the States do not have the proper papers.

A lot of gringo's are willing to apply for the proper papers but the 'dance' defeats them. This dance is like no other for there are many standard steps and then as the mood strikes them these clerks invent many 'new' steps just to see if you can stay on the floor and swing with them to these variations. Early on one clerk required that my wife and I submit 'certified' copies of our marriage license. No, a certificate from the Catholic Church was 'no good.' It must be from a civil authority, i.e., The County Recorders Office.

After we complied with this she then insisted that we bring two of our Mexican friends to stand in front of the Notario, swear and sign that we were, in fact, married and good people! Yep! We had to pay the notary.

Listen to those guys who say it was easy and realize that they have not been dancing long enough.

I mentioned my Catch-22 situation. Well, after many years of maintaining a bank account in Mexico (one of the dance steps) in my name I presented a copy of my latest bank statement, to prove we had the required $1500.00 in the bank, to a young female at the *Officina de Migration*. She shuffled my and my wives papers several times before she told me that my bank statement had to be dated within the past 30 days. Ok! Back to the bank to get a statement that was '30 days' new. Back to the clerk, lucky only an hour wait at the bank and she called my name after a mere 45 minutes. She, again, shuffled our papers. Finally she advised me that my papers were in order— BUT—that she could not renew my wives FM-3 because she was not on my bank account. Back to the Bank— where the guy took pity on me and took me out of the line to <u>help</u> me. What did I need, he asked. When I told him that I needed to add my wife to my account he said, *No problema*, just give me her FM-3 and I can do it in *dos minutos* (a couple of minutes). When I told him that was the problem he rolled his eyes to the sky, threw up his hands and said, "I am so sorry señor."

I lost my cool when I returned to discuss this with my friendly clerk. I started by addressing her as *"senora"* (she was a young senorita). I explained that I had been a guest of her gracious Country for many more years than she had been alive. I went on to call her a *'gringa.'* I explained that no true Mexican would deal with a 'guest' the way she was behaving toward my wife and me. I thought I had blown it when she stalked off. But no! She returned and handing me our FM-3's she said that she would overlook the problem—'this time.'

I definitely do not recommend that anyone follow my lead in this 'dance.' If you are really serious about being legal in Mexico—pay the middle man the money and let them process your papers—don't dance, just relax and have a drink!

It's true that the cost of renewing your FM-3 goes up each and every year. The good news is that you are 'allowed' to start the entire process over every five years forever or until you opt for trying to get an FM-2. I'll not even go there because now all of the paperwork must go through Mexico City. It normally requires an *Abogardo* (an attorney) and a few thousand dollars, U.S. The upside of an FM-2 is that you 'are allowed to work' (who wants to) in Mexico and after five years of renewals it then *may* be good for the rest of your life. Just think! No more dancing. Oh! Yes. The FM-2 gives you all of the rights of a natural citizen except that you may not vote nor may you serve in the Mexican military!

Now you ask: What is an FM-3?

Well, here goes—it is issued by *Estados Unidos Mexicanos Secretaria de Gobernacion as a Documento Migratorio del No Immigrante*! What does that mean I'm really not sure! The United States de Mexico by the Secretary of the Government issues it. It is a Document of Migration but not of Immigration It is good for five years— if you renew each year. It basically allows you to live within Mexico legally for a given period of time. I am fairly sure that it allows you access to the Court System within Mexico. Without it you are surely toast if you think you can fight your Mexican Landlord.

If you were paying attention you will understand why Mexicans get very upset when we refer to "America" as the "States." Sure you got it! They are the United States of Mexico but they do not have the hubris to refer to themselves as the "States."

Viva de Baile!

The Admiral and The Idiot

A few years back the people in La Salina became upset! No! They were just down right mad over the tremendous increase in off road vehicle activity on our beach. Good people were seriously talking about doing the riders' great bodily harm. The clowns were racing up and down in a continual cloud of dust accompanied by ear splitting noise from early morning and continuing uninterrupted until the wee hours of the following day. Not only was it impossible to sleep but even more importantly two children had been hospitalized as a result of being run over by drunken jerks who were just having fun. It had become unsafe for our kids to play on the beach! The folks were up in arms and looking for blood.

Several of us got together to discuss how we could go about returning our beach to its formerly quiet and safe character. We all agreed that I would contact the management of the Baja Seasons Trailer Park directly north of us. I sorta volunteered, you know, like McLaren did when he brought the cement mixer into camp. I talked with Ray Solis, the manager of the park, and we agreed that we would jointly ask for a meeting with the Admiral of the Fleet in Ensenada who has control of the Mexican Navy for all of Baja California. This would allow us to spell out our mutual problems with the off road vehicles and ask that he consider sending his Marines to deal with the problem. We agreed that Ray would contact the Admirals office and set up an appointment for the following week.

Ray was waiting for us when we pulled into camp the next Friday afternoon. He looked decidedly worried and not at all happy with the world. He explained that he had a phone call from the Admiral's aide who had informed him that he had better have himself and the crazy *gringo* (me) in his office by 8 o'clock Saturday morning. He told me that this was highly unusual for the "Admiral" to even bother to talk to a couple of *peones* (unskilled nobody's in this case) like us. I told him I would pick him up at 7 o'clock the next morning.

I didn't sleep much that night and by the looks of Ray he hadn't done any better. We discussed what we would say to the Admiral even though neither of us could figure why he was so mad at us. After all, we only wanted the Marines for a few hours to clear up the problem of illegal vehicles on the beach. We both became very uneasy as we pulled up in front of his headquarters in downtown Ensenada. The headquarters building was painted battleship gray. We noticed that the curb facing the drab building was empty of vehicles and that the civilians made

180

it a point to cross over to the other side of street rather than walk in front of the Navy Building. They were obviously avoiding the building.

Upon entering the building Ray introduced me to a Navy Chief at the front counter. He explained that we were there at the Admirals request. The Chief, in Spanish, corrected Ray saying that we were there on the 'orders' of the Admiral. When I asked Ray what he had said, he looked down at the floor and told me, "You don't really want to know." I insisted that he tell me and then I started to feel even more uncomfortable. The Chief pointed to two wooden chairs, right next to the 'brig', and told us to *Esperar* (wait) in a totally unfriendly manner. Two hours later we were still waiting. I asked to use the restroom and one of the sailors laughed, opened the steel door of the 'brig' and told me I could use the head inside. I politely declined even though I was about to float away.

The Chief came back and, in a very menacing manner, asked us why we had sent the *Jefe* (boss) a box full of old baseball equipment. We both looked at each other and then fell all over ourselves as we denied sending 'anything' to the *Jefe*. He then wanted to know about the letter we had sent demanding that the Marines be directed to take care of the beach problem. "WOW" we had not sent a letter. What was going on!

A short time later we were escorted into the Admirals office where we were left standing in front of his desk. He interrogated us through an interpreter. The Admiral an imposing, but short, officer who sported a gray 'crew cut' haircut, very unusual for a Mexican Military

Officer. Ray was in shock and had difficulty putting three words together. I would have been tongue tied if I had known what he did—that we might not be returning to camp. The *Jefe* could if he so chose to make us his guests for a long time. By the direction of the questioning it became obvious that he thought that we had tried to bribe him with 'old worn out baseball gloves and bats.' He was plainly angered by this. After standing for what seemed like a month, I explained that there had to be some mistake. I told him that I, as a Police Captain, had only the greatest respect for him, his Navy and the Marines. He relaxed a little, at one point I though that he was going to crush the edge of his desk, and gestured us into chairs next to his desk. His aide handed Ray a letter that was written in English. As I read it I found that some *other gringo idiot* from La Mision had written the letter and sent the worn out bribes to the Navy. When we finally got this cleared up; the Admiral smiled and quite politely, in perfect English, asked if there was anything that he could do to help us! Both Ray and I thanked him profusely and forgetting our problems with the beach we beat a hasty retreat from his office as fast as we could.

Stopping at the nearest Bar we ordered a couple of beers and I used the head. We celebrated our newly won freedom with a few more beers.

Damn those *gringo's* who don't know the Mexican people well enough to know when they have insulted them.

A few months later I was telling this story to a group of people in the Cantina when John Swete, a member of the camp and a retired United States Marine Aviator,

182

began laughing uncontrollably. It seems that he and the Admiral had both been pilots and that they had been close friends for years. John said the guy was a pussycat and I responded, "Bull Shit." John became our liaison with the Mexican Military until he moved to China where he had other military buddies.

God protect us from idiots!

Peacocks! In Baja?

Several years ago Charlie Carbahal, came by the house and asked me if I wanted to go on a picnic with him and Tequila Pancho. When I expressed interest he told me they would pick me up at 8 o'clock the next morning. He then proceeded to tell me what I was to bring. Two cases of beer, 5 kilos (11 pounds) of Carna Asada, and a cooler full of ice. He would bring the corn tortillas and Pancho would bring the Tequila. Fine!

Bright and early the next day they showed up in Charlie's Eagle, a four-wheel drive, Sedan. I told them I had all of my stuff but we would have to stop at the Butcher Shop in La Mision to get the streaks. On leaving the Mercado we headed east up the La Mision valley. We forded a stream, which they told me ran year round. Next we passed the giant water pumps, that tap the waters of the valley, the water is sent north to slack the thirsts of thousands of people in Tijuana. This system is an engineering marvel. The water is pumped out of the ground, sent about four miles west and then it is pumped up to the concrete tower on the mountain on the north side of the La Mision River. From this tower the water is gravity fed all the way to Tijuana. The system still provides much of the water for all of the settlements north of La Mision including Rosarito and parts of Tijuana. How do you make water flow, without any energy source, over hills and valleys for over 40 miles?

After crossing the stream we started to climb a very narrow road; it was just hanging on the side of the cliff. Only one lane wide it continually switched back and forth to reduce the steepness of the grade. Soon we were on top of a broad mesa and we began to encounter barbwire gates every few of miles.

Charlie explained that each time we passed through a gate we were moving from one ranch to another. You may not pass through these ranches without knowing the owners. We began to see huge old Oak Trees, dozens of cows were taking their mid day siesta away from the hot sun. There were more cows than I had ever seen in Baja.

On leaving the last gate we began to ascend a very steep and rutted track that wound up and around a mountain. Reaching the top, we rapidly dropped down into a beautiful valley. A small alpine lake greeted us. It was fed by a quietly bubbling artesian spring. The farmhouse had been built back in the 1870's. It had been a working

184

ranch for well over a hundred years. Horses and cows were housed in large, ram shackled, barns. Goats and a few pigs wandered all over the place.

I kept thinking this is not any part of Baja that I had ever seen. It was 'green'. Huge oak trees shaded the house and hovered over part of the pond. Approaching the house Charlie pulled over and stopped under a welcoming a shade tree. Pancho introduced us to his young nephew, Jamie (pronounced Hamie), and his wife. He explained that they were the caretakers of the ranch. Their three young kids were between the ages of three and six. They never stopped running, skipping and laughing.

Everywhere we walked we encountered chickens running underfoot. The place was right out of the "Old West." It was great!

As Charlie and I unloaded the car Pancho took a long pull on his tequila and offered Jamie a shot. He declined saying he would rather stick to the beer the rest of us were drinking. Pancho pulled a couple of six packs of sodas and a big bag of candy out for the kids. What a treat! They ate well at the ranch but they seldom get such wonderful treats. They both had a coke, and then a candy bar. This brought momma swooping down on them. She removed the rest of the goodies into the house for safekeeping.

Charlie gathered twigs and small branches and started a good fire. Pancho kicked a few rocks in a circle around the fire and the nephew placed the lid of a 55-gallon drum over the rocks. Out came the carne asada and tortillas. The steaks were placed on the old lid and they rapidly began to sizzle. The aroma had all of us drooling long before they were ready to eat. No utensils of any kind were used. When the meat had to be turned you grasped it with a tortilla and flipped it over. You moved fast to keep from burning your fingers. When the steaks were done you just rolled them up in a tortilla and chowed down. The beer flowed and Pancho showed how he got his nickname— 'Tequila Pancho.' We all eat until we were stuffed. We just lay back under that tree, relaxed, and took a short siesta.

Out from behind the closest barn came five of the biggest <u>peacocks</u> I have ever seen—the only other ones I have seen were in the San Diego Zoo. Pancho told us that a lot of the ranchers used them like guard dogs. They would attack anyone that didn't belong on the ranch. They would raise such a noise that the owner could get his gun and see what was what. They also ate all of the snakes that ventured into the ranch yard proper. An added advantage is that they don't have to be fed. They were fun to watch and when they spread their tail feathers they were spectacular.

We all wandered up to the pond to soak our feet. Charlie ended up trying his hand at fishing. He caught a mess of blue gill, which he gave to the lady of the house.

After a few more pulls on his bottle Pancho challenged me to a shoot off with his pistol. He knew that I was a San Diego cop and he figured that he could shoot better than me. Well, I am a pretty good shot and I made him look sad. We were shooting at cans lying on the ground. Jamie watched us for a while, and then he went into the house. He came out carrying the most pitiful looking .22 cal rifle I have ever seen. Part of the stock was broken and the ammo tube under the barrel was wired on with rusty old bailing wire. He smiled at us and off hand, shooting from the hip, shot the head off of a chicken

running full tilt across the yard. That guy could really shoot!

On our way back down the cliff we saw just how treacherous that road could be. A bunch of guys were using a farm tractor to pull a pickup out of the stream. The truck's roof had been caved in when it slid off the cliff.

A wonderful day; almost like a fairy tale! Peacocks in Baja. Who would have thought!

Disfrutar Baja!

Baja Beckons . . .

A hundred miles from nowhere
Just around the corner
New friends will greet you

Kick back and relax
Let things go
Your needs will be met

The Credo of Baja is
Friends are made fast
And mostly to last

No Hurry No Worry
Just kick back and

ENJOY!

About the Author

Bernie Swaim was born and raised in San Diego County.

He joined the San Diego Police Department in 1958 and a few, short, years later he was introduced to La Salina Del Mar, a small campo about 40 miles below the border in Baja, California.

He likes to say that he has been coming to Baja longer than most of the natives have been alive.

A retired Police Captain, he lives with his wife, Lu Ann, in La Salina, Baja California, and in San Diego County.

ORDER FORM

Caballero Publishing
PO Box 710411, Santee, CA 92072-0411
www.caballeropublishing.com
bernieswaim@caballeropublishing.com

Please send me _____ copies of "*Mi Baja No Hurry No Worry.*"

Price $14.95 per book.

Shipping and handling within the U.S. $4.00 per book. Add $2.00 for each extra book. If ordering four (4) or more books shipping and handling is FREE. Please add 7.75% tax for products shipped to California addresses.

Total enclosed _____ (check or money order only). Please allow 7 to 21 days for delivery.

Name: _____
Address: _____
City: _____ State:_____
Zip: _____
Country (if other than the U. S.): _____

If you have enjoyed this book please tell your friends or better yet send them a copy.

Look for my next book, "Bouncing Around Baja" which should be available early in 2003.

Thanks,
Bernie

(Form IB)